LESSONS

LESSONS
An
Autobiography

Dr. An Wang
with Eugene Linden

Addison-Wesley Publishing Company, Inc.
Reading, Massachusetts   Menlo Park, California
Don Mills, Ontario   Wokingham, England   Amsterdam
Sydney   Singapore   Tokyo   Madrid   Bogotá
Santiago   San Juan

Many of the designations used by manufacturers and sellers to distinguish their products are claimed as trademarks. Where those designations appear in this book and Addison-Wesley was aware of a trademark claim, the designations have been printed in initial caps (for example, Model 300).

Library of Congress Cataloging-in-Publication Data

Wang, An, 1920–
 Lessons, an autobiography.

 Includes index.
  1. Wang, An, 1920– . 2. Wang Laboratories, Inc.
—History. 3. Computer industry—United States—
History. 4. Industrialists—United States—Biography.
I. Linden, Eugene. II. Title.
HD9696.C62A3 1986   338.7'61004'0924 [B]   86-10768
ISBN 0-201-09400-2

Jacket photograph by George W. DiSario/Wang Laboratories, Inc.
Cover design by Renfer Mayr
Text design by Lisa de Francis
Set in 12-point Garamond No. 3 by DEKR Corporation, Woburn, MA

ABCDEFGHIJ-MU-89876
First printing, August 1986

To my righteous Father
and my affectionate Mother and
to her Mother, Brothers, and
Sisters, who nurtured my youth
and growth

The master said:

"To learn and at due times to repeat
what one has learned, is that not,
after all, a pleasure?"

—Opening of the Lun Yü, *one of the
greatest of Confucian classics*

Contents

I would like to acknowledge the many people who have helped me in my life and who helped bring this project to fruition.

In particular, I want to thank my teachers—both in China and in America. To those who helped me learn in the classroom, I owe much of the technical skill and knowledge which became the foundation of my career. To those who helped me learn in the world beyond the classroom, I owe much of my success.

Above all, I want to thank the people who have worked with me at Wang Laboratories. To a large degree my story is also their story. In this book I have been able to mention only a few of them by name, but their talent and effort represent the talent and effort of the thousands of individuals who have built our organization.

I would also like to thank the members of the Wang community who dealt with the logistical problems of researching and writing this book. Paul Guzzi and Ed Pignone cleared all impediments that might have delayed its completion. Stasia Lyons managed the many drafts that were generated in the course of the project. Nancy Houghton and Rita Conlon facilitated the scheduling of interviews and meetings. Paul McCauley made sure that the technological apparatus was in place to complete the project.

In addition, I would like to thank Theresa Burns, whose editorial talents helped bring this book to fruition.

Finally, it should be noted that the proceeds from the publication of this book will go directly to the Wang Institute of Graduate Studies, an independent institution of higher learning.

Introduction

I find it somewhat surprising that so many talented people derail
themselves one way or another during their lives. People fail to
accomplish what they set out to do, or if they do accomplish
something, all too often a meteoric rise triggers a precipitous fall.
Of course, there is a strong element of luck in both success and
failure, but it is my belief that there are no "secrets" to success.
People fail for the most part because they shoot themselves in the
foot. If you go for a long time without shooting yourself in the
foot, other people start calling you a genius. But if there is
anything that compelled me to write this book, it is to show that
success is more a function of consistent common sense than of
genius.

I came to this country forty-one years ago from China. During
the years since, America and American business have passed
through several transformations, including the emergence of the
United States as the world leader in high technology following
World War II. I have played a small role in this era. As a
researcher at the Harvard Computation Laboratory in the late
1940s, I helped develop magnetic memory cores, which were

essential to the development of modern computers. Later I became a businessman seeking to find and market applications of my innovations in digital electronics.

In the thirty-five years since I founded Wang Laboratories, the company has grown from a one-man shop to an almost three-billion-dollar multinational company that employs over thirty thousand people. It has also changed from a company that produced specialized digital equipment for government, scientific laboratories, and industry into a company whose products bring the power of computers into every corner of the office. Throughout these transitions, the company has continued to grow at an average compounded rate of 42 percent.

Over the years, the financial community came to take this kind of growth for granted, and the company has often been singled out as an exemplar of long-term planning. However, as anyone in business knows, earnings growth can never be taken for granted, over the long term, the medium term, or the short term. As markets change and a company grows, it must adapt, and the transitions necessary for adaptation are not always smooth, even if from a distance growth looks smooth and continuous.

When I founded the company, I never expected that it would grow to its present size. Nor did I look thirty-five years down the road and foresee the unfolding of the computer era. I knew that it would be foolhardy to attempt to predict the distant future. Progress does not follow a straight line; the future is not a mere projection of trends in the present. Rather, it is revolutionary (which is why we speak of the computer revolution). It overturns the conventional wisdom of the present, which often conceals or ignores the clues to the future. In the late 1940s, when I was doing my research on magnetic core memory, the conventional wisdom was that a few large computers might satisfy all imaginable computer needs. While this may seem amusing and short-sighted from the vantage point of the present, it reflected the views of such eminent people as computer pioneer Howard Aiken, who looked at society and the economy and came to what they believed was a sensible conclusion.

While the computer revolution has produced an enormous industry, few of its commercial pioneers shared in this success. At any given moment in this revolution, the future was shrouded in uncertainty. A number of pioneers made the humbling discovery that technological wizardry did not necessarily translate into an understanding of markets and society—and the way both change. Technology does not stand apart from society; each is constantly affecting the shape of the other.

Given this revolutionary nature of the future, I have come to see that the key to long-term survival for a company is adaptability. One can sense change even if one doesn't know where it will ultimately lead. This does not mean looking decades into the future, but instead taking a clear-eyed look at the present and anticipating human needs in three or perhaps five years.

Because in technology I have always been driven by society's needs, I have been able to adapt. In technology, this means delivering solutions rather than computers. Just as an automobile dealer does not ask a customer to study automotive engineering, a computer firm should not demand that its customers learn about computers. Most people do not want to study computer science any more than a commuter wants to study the internal combustion engine. On the other hand, if a machine makes their work more efficient and less of a chore, they will be interested, and they will not really care whether or not the machine is called a computer.

At various points in my company's history, we have been well positioned both to discover and to take advantage of opportunities as they arose. This is to some degree the result of luck, but it is also the result of the decisions I made at every stage of our growth—about technology, products, management, and finance. Because I had no formal training in any of these fields with the exception of engineering, I had to learn to meet each challenge of managing a business as it arose.

My approach to management has been quite simple. At each stage of the growth of Wang Laboratories, I acquired the knowledge necessary to manage the next stage of growth. To grow faster than that, or to undertake projects that you are not yet prepared for, is to court disaster. I never really wanted Wang Laboratories to grow faster than 50 percent annually, because in any given year, I felt that I could only learn to manage a company 50 percent larger than the one I was then managing. With each small challenge I met, I was better prepared and more confident about my ability to meet a slightly greater challenge during the next phase of growth.

Today I have the luxury of looking back and analyzing what lay behind this approach. One thing I have discovered is that attitudes and values that I acquired in China long before I came to the United States have had a great bearing on the way I do business. These values have much in common with some of the virtues of Confucianism, the system of Chinese thought that stresses proper behavior and moderation. However, although I respect the spirit of Confucianism, I have not tried to adapt this ancient Chinese philosophy to modern America. I have not tried to devise a system at all.

Behind my decision-making process there lie certain attributes or virtues which I believe play a role in the success or failure of a business. Perhaps the most important of these is simplicity. I am not a fan of convoluted arguments or explanations. No matter how intricate a technological or scientific problem is, it can usually be reduced to a simple, comprehensible form. In my own specialty, electronics, the simplest solution is usually the best solution.

In the same way, even though a problem facing a businessman might seem incredibly complex and involve many variables, usually, upon contemplation, it will resolve into a simpler form and the key variable will emerge. In 1971, when I decided that we had to get out of the electronic calculator business, everybody around me was concerned with such things as market share, maintaining our competitive position, and our revenue stream. I was focused on the strategic implications of plummeting prices as semiconductor integrated circuits made their presence felt. Quite simply, I could see that calculators were becoming a commodity in the sense that people could now shop among brands on the basis of price rather than performance. I felt that we were not the best-positioned firm to compete in a commodity market. While the decision was not obvious, it was simple once one looked past the clutter.

Besides simplicity, other things I have found to be essential to success are communication, moderation and patience, adaptability, decisiveness, confidence, unconventional thinking, social responsibility, and last, but by no means least, luck. The importance of these attributes is in their interaction. Some of them are antithetical to others—patience will often collide with decisiveness, for instance—and yet it is hard to think of any of my decisions in which they did not play a role.

If any one concept emerges from the interplay of these traits, it is that of balance—very much a Confucian ideal. Balance is really nothing more than an orientation that gives you a sense of where you are in any given situation. It is what prevents you from getting so caught up in the pressures of the moment that you lose sight of where you are going and what must be done. It is what tempers decisiveness so that it does not lead to dictatorship. It is what tempers confidence so that a useful trait does not become a dangerous one.

Perhaps the hardest thing for an aggressive person to learn is to rein his instincts in the interests of long-term success. I did not found a computer company in 1951. The huge expense of such an enterprise made it an impractical idea. It was not until nearly two decades later that the company had evolved to the point where designing and building a computer was a logical thing for Wang Laboratories to do. By then we had the resources, the marketing skills, and the stability to embark on an undertaking of this scale.

Today the high-tech marketplace is an intensely competitive arena, and a number of entrepreneurs who left the shelter of major corporations or academia to set out on their own have discovered that it is not enough to have a good idea, or even a good product, in order to start a corporation that will survive amid the giants of domestic and foreign competition. This has produced a counterreaction of sorts, in which once again people are beginning to argue that without specialized expertise in marketing, management, and finance as well as technological prowess, the lone amateur cannot make it.

I do not think this is so. Surely the situation today poses no greater challenges than I faced when I started a business as a recent immigrant to this country. Change itself continually creates opportunities for those who recognize its importance, whether they are inside or outside the establishment. One does not have to be a specialist to succeed, and perhaps more important, one does not have to come from a particular class or ethnic group or political party. I discovered that with some common sense and discipline, I could compete and succeed in what was at first an alien society. I discovered that I could do this without leaving my values behind me when I went to work in the morning. I certainly made mistakes along the way, but even then, I found that I could minimize their consequences and turn them into lessons from which something positive might come.

I offer readers of this book the proposition that there is no magic in mastering the challenges of starting and nurturing a business, even in an arena as esoteric as high technology. One can succeed without being possessed of prophetic powers. One can prosper without getting an MBA, or being bullied by MBAs, or succumbing to the management fads that periodically capture the attention of America's boardrooms. I also believe that the approach to business I am describing might benefit people in any number of occupations. I hope therefore that these pages will not be read as a catalog of my achievements but rather as a case study of one man making decisions and taking risks. The landscape of society and business has changed since I started out, and it will continue to change, but the opportunities remain for those who choose to seize them.

I
Preparation

1
The Age
of Confusion

I was born in the middle of what has been called the Age of Confusion—the struggle for the soul of China after centuries of medieval rule. The bloodshed of this struggle, and later the Japanese invasion of my homeland, disrupted every aspect of my childhood. It was a time of complete uncertainty, not just for me and my family but for the institutions and ideas that had previously defined China.

The China of the 1920s and 1930s was not the China of contemplation and delicate arts that Americans sometimes picture. It was a China of feuding warlords and corruption, of Japanese brutality and fear. While some people seek out risks to test themselves, I did not have to look far to find either challenge or calamity. Both were impossible to avoid.

During these upheavals, I lost both of my parents and one sister. Even before their deaths, I had been separated from my family for most of a decade, often forced to take on more responsibility than my years would ordinarily require. From a very early age, I discovered that I could succeed at tasks that other people did not think I was old enough to accomplish; I learned to negotiate my way in unfamiliar territory. I became a loner by circumstance, not by choice, but the discovery that I could survive and even thrive on my own gave me confidence.

I have come to believe that confidence is sometimes rooted in the unpleasant, harsh aspects of life, and not in warmth and safety. It is an intangible quality, but it has its own momentum. The longer you survive and succeed, the better able you are to further survive and succeed.

When I came to the United States at age twenty-five, I knew that even in a world of confusion I could find my way.

I was born in Shanghai, China, on February 7, 1920. My name, An Wang, means "Peaceful King." I was the eldest son, one of five children. My older sister, Hsu, died—I never knew how exactly—in 1945 during the Japanese invasion. I also have a younger sister named Yu, and two brothers, Ping and Ge. Yu is six years younger than I, Ping is ten years younger, and Ge is fourteen years younger. Because I went off to school at age thirteen, I did not have the time to form deep attachments to my brothers and sisters, who, with the exception of Hsu, were so very much younger than I.

We were middle class. My father taught English in a private elementary school in Kun San about thirty miles from Shanghai. From time to time, when school was disrupted by war or civil strife, he practiced traditional Chinese medicine, which made him a figure of respect in our community. This kind of doctoring dates back thousands of years and involves the use of herbs and other organic substances to treat common ailments such as stomach upset, flu, and malaria. In those days, it was the only medicine available to ordinary Chinese. And yet, in most cases, it was effective, and these doctors functioned much as general practitioners do in America.

My father was well educated for his time. He had spent a year at Chiao Tung University (now Jiao Tong University), the university I later attended. At the time he went to Chiao Tung, very few Chinese went to college, so even though he studied for only one year, he was still far better educated than most in our small city.

As a man, my father was taciturn and intimidating, a disciplinarian. Later on, though, I would discover that he showed affection through gestures rather than words. My mother's personality was the exact opposite of my father's. She was loving and indulgent, not at all strict.

Like many Chinese families, we had a written history which would be updated every couple of generations by an affluent member of the family. These books gave our families a sense of continuity and permanence that I don't see in the more mobile West. It was only a few years ago that I acquired a copy of this book, but I recall my father pointing it out on a bookshelf when I was a child. It claims to be accurate for twenty-three generations, back to the time of the Mongol invasion and Marco Polo's trip to China. With less certainty, the history goes back another twenty-five generations. We never quite trusted the earlier twenty-five generations because the county magistrate from whom the modern genealogy descends had moved a thousand miles to take his post. Even so, like most Chinese children, I grew up with a sense that my culture and my family had been around for a very long time.

Until I was twenty-one, I lived either in Shanghai or in Kun San, where my father's ancestors had lived for six hundred years. The area where I grew up is one of the most fertile and strategically important parts of China. Shanghai, which in Chinese means "By the Sea," controls the mouth of the Yangtze River, which carries trade from a thousand miles inside China to the sea. If you wanted to dominate China, you had to control Shanghai. This is one of the reasons the city was the site of almost perpetual conflict during my childhood.

Kun San, a city of about ten thousand people, lies about thirty miles upstream from Shanghai, on the rich soil carried down by the Yangtze. In ancient times it was well protected. A moat encircled the central part of the city, and inside the moat was a wall ten feet high and fifteen feet thick. Centuries later, the wall was broken up and used to make a peripheral road around the city, but the moat and some of the wall's ruins remain today. The formerly walled part of the town is crisscrossed with canals on which gondolalike boats drift, carrying fish and other goods within the city.

In the northern corner of Kun San is a three-hundred-foot-high hill (the word *san* means "hill" in Chinese) which my friends and I used to climb. The hill is composed of unusual minerals deposited by the Yangtze, and it is overgrown with bushes and flowers. Along the paths that climb to the top are rest areas and lookouts with pagoda-style roofs. The climate in Kun San is temperate, a little warmer than Boston's, and the area produces all manner of vegetables. We never suffered from the droughts and famines that plagued the rest of China. Until I was older, I did not know of the hardships described by Pearl Buck in *The Good Earth*.

In all, by the time I was thirteen we had lived in four different houses. The first was a rented house in Shanghai that was part of a compound owned by my mother's family. During this time, my father remained in Kun San to teach, and so until I was six, I saw him only on weekends. The compound in Shanghai was walled, and there was not much space for a garden. Our house had two levels, with the living rooms and kitchen downstairs and the bedrooms upstairs. It was not luxurious, but it was comfortable, and we each had a room of our own. I was grateful for this, for even as a child, I valued privacy.

I never knew my grandfathers, as both died in my infancy, but I saw my grandmothers often. Ordinarily in China, children spend more time with their paternal grandmothers, but because we lived in my mother's family's compound until I was six, I grew up without any notion that traditionally the maternal side of the family had a lower status. My grandmothers lived within a block of each other, and I have to say that I chose to visit the one I thought would give me the most sweets.

While I was concerned with the fastest way to get at the sweets, the world outside our neighborhood was being torn apart. China's first attempt at democracy had failed before I was born, and Shanghai was the scene of a continuing struggle between the groups that warred for control. The political events of the day were constantly discussed by my parents and their friends, though at the time I understood little about what was going on.

During these years, China was largely ruled by warlords who took advantage of the naiveté of Sun Yat-sen, who was briefly the president of the Chinese republic. The living symbol of democracy in China, Sun was a high-minded revolutionary who spent much of his time in Europe and the United States trying to gain support for his cause. In fact, when the Revolution of 1911 started, Sun was in the United States. He and his followers were never very worldly, and while they talked about democratic principles, the warlords carved up China into separate kingdoms they could rule.

For the Chinese people, emerging from generations of decadent dynastic rule, the idea of democracy—that a person might choose his own leaders and that he might rise according to his energy and ability—was like the light that blinds the man emerging from a cave. People like Sun Yat-sen were so entranced by the nobility of their mission that they were easy prey for the warlords, who quickly saw the power vacuum created by the fall of the imperial government of the Manchu. The rivalries of the warlords produced famines in the countryside, and continual bloodshed in the cities.

When I was growing up, the Nationalist Party (or Kuomintang) was scheming, dealing, and fighting to establish itself as the dominant political organization in China. It was the Kuomintang who eventually subdued or bought off the warlords, but even after that, the purges and power struggles continued.

Although most Americans think of the Kuomintang as the power base of Chiang Kai-shek during his long war with the Communists, political alliances were as confusing as everything else during this era, and for a period in the 1920s, the Communists and the Kuomintang were allies. In fact, Chiang was assisted by Russian advisors in 1926, when he finally subdued the warlords during his northern expedition.

Once Chiang had established control over the warlords, he no longer needed the Communists, and in April 1927, he turned against them after forming a secret alliance with the bankers and merchants of Shanghai. He used local underworld gangs—who were his allies—to round up and slaughter the Communist Party members in the city. It was episodes like this that caused the period to be called the Age of Confusion.

For some educated Chinese, this period was like the European Renaissance, but for most of the poor, the times were more like the Dark Ages. Europeans read about the Dark Ages in textbooks as ancient history. The Age of Confusion is a living, terrible memory to those who suffered through it.

We had moved to Kun San in 1926, the year before the northern expedition reached Shanghai, but we felt its effects. During the bloody split between the Nationalists and the Communists, my parents sheltered an uncle of mine who had at one time been a leftist. I could not understand what crime he had committed, but his fear spoke of the terrors of the world outside our small city. My uncle remained hidden in our house in Kun San for the next six months, until the danger passed. Had he been caught, the chances are he would have suffered the fate of other leftists, who were shot or subjected to more brutal forms of killing such as beheading and slow strangulation.

The move to Kun San had a profound effect on my life, but for reasons unrelated to politics. In 1926, I was old enough to begin school, but the private elementary school where my father taught English had no kindergarten or first or second grades. So I began my schooling as a third-grader, and for the rest of my education in China, I remained two years younger than my classmates. This put me at a great disadvantage with respect to my classmates, but I think there were benefits to being out of my depth. It is a little bit like being thrown in the water when you don't know how to swim. You either learn how to swim—and fast—or you sink. You might hate the unpleasantness of the experience, but you gain a little confidence in your ability to deal with difficult situations. Being thrown into the third grade at the age of six was not my choice, but I found that with some struggling I could handle both the work and the social pressures.

When you are young and find yourself in unusual circumstances, almost every event takes on a heightened significance. I remember that when I was six and walking home from school one day, I came upon a bird's nest that had fallen out of a tree. The nest had a baby sparrow in it. I wanted to keep the bird, so I took the nest with its chirping baby sparrow home with me. A little nervous, I decided to leave the nest outside until I had told my parents what I had found, but it took me a while to get up the nerve to talk to them. As a six-year-old, I knew nothing about the peculiar relationship between cats and birds, so when I went outside again, I was dumbfounded to find that the bird had disappeared. Even though I did not know about cats, I knew that my failure to bring the bird in immediately had probably cost the poor thing its life. It was my first lesson in the importance of acting rather than hesitating.

I discovered early on that I was good at math. I found that the answers to math problems would come to me if I thought about them long and hard enough. I remember one embarrassing moment after an exam when I was about ten. The arithmetic teacher held up my exam and another boy's and said to him, "Here is a boy who is two years younger than you, and yet his exam score is close to one hundred, and here is your test, whose score could be counted on the fingers of one hand." Needless to say, this is not the kind of attention that makes a younger, smaller boy popular with his classmates.

While math was easy for me, I had some difficulty keeping up in history, geography, and other subjects that were taught by means of rote memorization. It was not the subject matter but the tedious teaching method that bored me. I realized then that I could discipline myself to concentrate on subjects that interested me, but to this day I have a hard time concentrating on ones— such as political doctrine—that don't.

Except for the emphasis on Chinese history and culture, my schooling was probably not very different from an American child's at that time. Those years gave me a very good foundation for the more sophisticated subjects I studied later on. Besides history and math, I also studied English, a compulsory subject from the fourth grade onward. I had a bit of a head start here because my father was an English teacher: when I was four, he had begun to teach me the English alphabet at home.

Perhaps because fewer children in China actually go to school than in the United States, I think the Chinese place a much higher value on elementary education than do Americans. It has always surprised me, in fact, to see how little respect elementary-schoolteachers in America get from the academic community and the general public.

Outside of school, my father's mother took it upon herself to instruct me in Chinese literature and thought. At first, these sessions were like Sunday school—the texts went in one ear and out the other. I was more interested in the sweets I knew would come at the end of the lesson than I was in what the lesson taught.

But my grandmother was as diligent in tutoring me as she had been with my father, and eventually some information began to sink in. It was during these hours with her that I learned about Confucianism, the practical philosophy that has profoundly influenced Chinese character.

For twenty-five hundred years, Confucianism has evolved in many different ways—some of them seemingly contradictory—but its essence might be described as a combination of the golden rule and the notion of moderation and balance. Periodically Confucianism has gone into decline, as it did during the Age of Confusion. This cycle has repeated itself throughout Chinese history: a long period of stable bureaucratic rule is disrupted by a revolutionary period, when conventional wisdom is challenged. Confucian ideas dominate the stable periods and then become obscured during the revolutionary periods. But even Mao Tse-tung found that he could not rid China of Confucianism. It is too deeply embedded in China's soul.

Thanks to my grandmother, it is deeply embedded in mine as well. Just as many of the attributes or principles that I feel are important to success in business—such as moderation, patience, balance, and simplicity—are Confucian in spirit, so is my belief that a sense of satisfaction comes from service to one's community.

As I finished the sixth grade, we had to decide whether I should take the exam to go on to junior high school or wait a year to reduce the age difference between myself and my classmates. In China at that time, admission to a public junior high school was based on a competitive exam. But even if you were accepted, your family still had to pay. I recall that the fee for the first semester was ten silver dollars—a considerable sum for a family in China in the 1930s. There were just two junior high schools in Kun San, and they had to serve a district of a couple of hundred thousand people. Together they only had places for between fifty and a hundred students each year. Because my grades in nonscientific subjects were not good—indeed, I had barely managed to graduate from elementary school—my parents encouraged me to wait a year before taking the exam.

I was absolutely sure, however, that I did not want to repeat the sixth grade. And so I took the test despite my parents' wishes. When the results came back, it turned out that I had scored the highest of any of the applicants. My parents promptly forgot about my disobedience—they were delighted with the results. My father was not a man to express his pride in words, but I understood his willingness to pay the ten silver dollars as a gesture of great affection.

This was just a small triumph, but confidence is cumulative. Although my grades were bad, and my age was a handicap, I was sure I could do well on the exam. I turned out to be right, and this made me believe that I could rise to the occasion in other situations as well.

When I got into junior high school, I again did poorly in the humanities courses. Once I had passed the exam, I reverted to my former study habits, which had more to do with finding reasons to play than they did with spending long hours on home-work. I promptly flunked several courses, and it looked as though my happiness was going to be short-lived. But since I had done exceptionally well in mathematics, I was permitted to take sum-mer school courses, and then to take another examination in the fall. Once again, I set about to concentrate. I passed this exam—though just barely—and was allowed to continue in school. This established a pattern that was to be repeated a few more times. While I was not the most diligent student, I could always do well enough on exams to get by.

Although I was bored by some of my courses, I was still an avid reader. Kun San had a small library, and I regularly spent my afternoons reading every type of book. My first love, however, was the sciences, particularly physics and mathematics. I read about Leonardo da Vinci, Galileo, and many of the other thinkers of Western science. I remember being very impressed by reading an account of Isaac Newton's life and his discovery of gravity. Here was someone who could look past the conventional wisdom and see something that no one else could see, even though what he was seeing—gravity—is among the most obtrusive facts of life. I liked the idea of questioning concepts that people generally accepted unconditionally. Although Kun San was anything but cosmopolitan—I don't think that there were any non-Chinese living there at the time—by reading I learned a lot about the world beyond my town and even beyond China.

While I was in junior high school, in the early 1930s, the Nationalist government was in control, but just barely. The riots and fighting of the 1920s still flared up now and then, and any good news on the domestic front was overshadowed by the ominous movements of the Japanese, who began to look at China the way a cat looks at an untended Thanksgiving turkey. Although China and Japan were not yet at war, in 1931 the Japanese seized Manchuria and repeatedly bombed Shanghai.

Talk of Japan now replaced the domestic struggles as the topic of the day. As the newspapers reported on the daily maneuverings of the Japanese, politicians trooped through our school to give political lectures we were forced to attend. We also had to participate in mass rallies at which speakers would inflame the crowd against the Japanese, and occasionally the British. Between the ages of eight and twelve, I was forced to join about five rallies a year. Listening to these presumably stirring speeches, I became deeply disenchanted with politics. It seemed to me that the more eloquent the speaker, the less likely it was that he would practice what he preached. These compulsory meetings turned me against political activism, and I never became caught up in the political fervor of the time.

There were, however, things that did excite me. In junior high school, I founded a student newspaper, my first exposure to the problems of typesetting. Though it lasted only two issues, it started me thinking about publishing. Two decades later, my early interest in typesetting and publishing resurfaced in my own business.

When I was thirteen, I started at Shanghai Provincial High School, just a few blocks from my grandparents' house. It had one of the best academic reputations in China—like the Bronx High School of Science in New York City. In fact, the principal had earned his master's degree under the supervision of the famed American educator John Dewey, at Columbia University. We used the same algebra text in high school that a number of American colleges used for freshman courses. My geography and history books were also written in English, and so my lack of interst in memorizing dates and the names of places was compounded by the difficulties of having to memorize them in English.

Not long after I enrolled, the school moved ten miles out of Shanghai. From that point on, I boarded at the school and lived apart from my family. Our days were strictly regimented. Classes ended at around four o'clock, we were given two hours to study after dinner, and the lights went out promptly at nine. Though I was not very happy with the routine, being forced to use American textbooks left me well prepared when I later came to the United States.

One casualty of my age disadvantage was participation in organized sports. Because I was so much smaller than my classmates, I really could not take part in team sports (although I did occasionally serve as a goalie—really more of a target—in soccer). I discovered, however, that I could play individual sports such as table tennis, where my larger classmates did not have so marked an advantage. In fact, years later, I became good enough to compete on my university team.

Upon graduation from high school at the age of sixteen, I was accepted by Chiao Tung University in Shanghai. At that time, Chiao Tung was perhaps the most prestigious of China's universities. It was the MIT of China. Because I had the highest college entrance exam scores of my class, I was made class president, an office I held for the next four years. I studied electrical engineering with an emphasis on communications, and I found the work easy. I liked electrical engineering because it involved practical applications of math and physics, my favorite subjects. In truth, I spent more time competing at table tennis and perfecting my game than I did studying engineering.

I was anything but idle, however. Among the projects I took on was the chore of editing a scientific digest of sorts. My job was to look through American magazines such as *Popular Mechanics* and *Popular Science* for interesting articles, which I would then translate into Chinese. While this might seem like a normal enough thing for an American student to do, in China it would have been radical only a couple of generations earlier. Although I never became caught up in politics, many of my favorite teachers in high school had been activists in the struggle to turn China into a modern society, and their taste for Western democracy and science influenced me. The goal of these teachers was not to shun Chinese culture at all, but rather to open the country up to new ideas and technology. They were trying to show that we could learn from the world beyond China's borders. This was the positive side of the Age of Confusion.

During my freshman year in college, talk focused on the Japanese, and whether the Nationalists were doing enough to oppose them. Japan had seized Manchuria in 1931, and it had become ever more belligerent toward China. There was no way China could match the military might of Japan, and Chiang wavered between toughness and compromise. At one point, Chiang was kidnapped and briefly held under house arrest by one of his own generals, part of the faction who felt that Chiang's policies would lead to the ruin of China.

Just a few days after I had heard about the kidnapping of Chiang, I received far more devastating news from Kun San. My mother's health had declined during the past few years, and now she was dead. While she had not been a victim of the street violence or Japanese bombings, she had been broken by years of fear and conflict. In short, she was a victim of the times.

While Japan committed acts of war against China during most of the 1930s, World War II did not officially start for China until Japan seized Peking in 1937 and then began to march south. The Japanese later launched a separate thrust from Shanghai westward to Nanking, the capital.

At that time, Shanghai consisted of a large Chinese city and what were called the concessions: a nine-square-mile area that was divided up into two large areas, the International Settlement, which was governed by the British, the Americans, and other foreign concession holders, and the French concession, which was governed by the French. China had been forced to grant the concessions to the Western powers following the first Opium War (1839–1842). Although the concessions were on Chinese soil, they were treated as foreign territory. In a concession, a Chinese was a foreigner in his own city and subject to the regulations of whatever interest governed his district. When war came to Shanghai, the humiliating status of the concessions turned out to be something of a blessing.

After the spring term of 1937, I had gone home to Kun San for summer vacation between my freshman and sophomore years. The threat of war was very much in the air, and by July, after only a few weeks at home, I realized that if I did not get back to Shanghai quickly, I might not be able to get back to Shanghai at all. So with the approval of my father, I packed up and returned to the university. The instinct that prompted me to return served me well, because the bloody march on Nanking began just a couple of weeks after the invasion of Shanghai in August 1937. At the time I returned, Chiao Tung University was outside the International Settlement. But after the invasion by Japan, the government decided to move the university to leased buildings inside the French concession for safety. For the first few years of the war, the Japanese respected the territorial integrity of the concessions so as not to incite the Americans (or the French or the British) to enter the war.

Of the thirty students in my class, only fifteen made it back to school that year. The remainder were separated from the concession by Japanese troops. But during the course of the following year, most of them were able to make their way back.

Thus, there was war all around me, but not in the nine square miles within which I spent the next three years. We could hear Japanese shells whistling overhead from time to time, but even though the war was close by, it was not there, and that made all the difference in the world. I could not venture beyond the concession without falling into the hands of the Japanese, but nine square miles is large enough so that this confinement was not a hardship.

Because I was in the international zone, I was very well informed about the progress of the war, particularly about the atrocities the Japanese were committing. During the twenties, different factions of Chinese had been murdering each other, but the presence of an outside enemy had the effect of uniting these factions. Still, the ten divisions of Japanese made mincemeat of the poorly organized opposition as they swept through Shanghai to Nanking. In Nanking, which Chiang abandoned to the Japanese, their armies massacred 300,000 people, many more than were killed in the American atomic bombings of Hiroshima and Nagasaki.

The numbers were only part of the horror. The Japanese seemed to put a great deal of energy into inventing the most sadistic forms of torture and murder. One method they used was to bury men up to their necks and douse their heads with boiling water. The rape of the city went on for two months after all resistance ceased. It was later established that the hideous sporting events the troops invented to relieve the monotony of mass executions were the result of a Japanese policy decision to inflict the maximum horror and humiliation on the Chinese, and not the excesses of undisciplined troops.

Although those of us within the concession were relatively safe, we heard daily reports of these atrocities and could only imagine what was happening to our families. Abandoned by our own armies, we were powerless to do anything about the slaughter. And so I felt incredible relief and joy when I learned that my family had made its way into the concession from Kun San, which had not felt the full brunt of the Japanese terror.

Ironically, the fortunes of the Chinese within the concession were tied to the war in Europe. Bad news on the Western Front was bad news for us because, with every Nazi victory, the Japanese tightened their noose on the international zone in Shanghai. After the fall of France in 1940 and the installation of the Vichy Government, the French could no longer resist Japanese demands that gave them ever-increasing authority in the French concession. And with the British preoccupied with the blitzkrieg, Churchill was not in any position to take a strong stand against Japanese encroachments on British interests. In fact, for all his opposition to appeasement in Europe, Churchill was at first conciliatory to the Japanese in Asia.

Japanese control of the French concessions in China cost the Chinese army one of its principal supply routes. We were left with only the Burma Road, which was under the control of the British. Right after Dunkirk, Churchill sent an olive branch to the Japanese by agreeing to forbid its use as a Chinese supply line. One of the things I have always admired President Franklin D. Roosevelt for is his refusal to budge in his support of China, even before Pearl Harbor.

After being graduated from Chiao Tung in 1940, I spent the next year at the university as a teaching assistant in electrical engineering. But it was becoming clear that the Japanese would soon control all of Shanghai. I also felt that it was time I made my contribution to the war effort. In the summer of 1941, about eight of my classmates and I signed on for the project that would best use our skills: designing and building transmitters and radios for the government troops for the Central Radio Corporation, an installation in the interior of China. We did this through the university, whose alumni included some of China's biggest industrialists. The decision to join up was again a lucky one: only a few months later, Japan attacked Pearl Harbor, after which there were no more safe havens in Shanghai for either Chinese or foreigners.

My fellow volunteers and I took a boat from Shanghai to Hong Kong. There we were instructed to make our way to Kweilin, deep in the mainland. To get there, we traveled to Kuang-chou-wan, a French concession on a peninsula not far from the Yellow Sea. At this point, hundreds of miles from Shanghai, the Japanese lines were stretched thin. Our group infiltrated through the lines by cover of nightfall and marched for three days before we felt it was safe to travel openly. We then took a riverboat and a train into the interior of China.

When I arrived in Kweilin, I was put in charge of a group designing radio equipment to be used in the war. I was twenty-one, and the job had a fair amount of responsibility. My work supported the military, but I was not really living a military life. It was a seat-of-the-pants operation with the spirit of a start-up. We got news about allied technological breakthroughs from articles that would come with the mail on lend-lease air transports, our only link to the outside world. We were never certain which radio parts would be available, or when we would be stymied by a shortage of critical components. For instance, we had to invent a hand-powered generator to run a mobile radio transmitter needed by the troops. Because different people would turn the handles that powered the generator at different rates, we also had to invent a way of ensuring that the voltage was constant no matter how fast the handles were cranked. We got a lot of practice in the scavenging and improvisation that you often have to do when you're trying to design some new machine.

Despite the entrepreneurial atmosphere of our operation, we never forgot that there was a war going on. Bombing raids continued to come once or twice a week. We were a favorite target of the Japanese because of our manufacturing importance to the Chinese army. When the bombers were sighted, the sentries sounded an alarm, and we would drop what we were doing and scramble to the caverns in nearby mountains. The din was alarming at first, but we quickly realized that the caves were deep enough to be invulnerable. While the bombs dropped outside, we would pass the time by playing cards. The others in my group were also former college students, and contract bridge was the game of choice while we waited out the bombers.

Although I did not know this until much later, not long after I left Shanghai to join the war effort, my father died. I do not know precisely how he died, only that it was a result of the war. So many people were killed during the war that it was often impossible to piece together exactly what had happened. With my mother also dead, I was truly on my own. My older sister Hsu had married in 1941 and was living with her new husband's family. My younger sister and brothers had been taken in by other relatives. Fortunately (with the exception of Hsu) they all survived the war, although I did not have a chance to see them again for forty years.

My years in the interior were eye-opening for me because it was the first time I witnessed the tyranny inflicted on the peasants by the local Chinese generals. The area around Kweilin was poor, and even the war with Japan did not keep corrupt military men and provincial officials from squeezing people to the point of starvation. As the war went on, the discipline of the armies broke down, and the generals became ever more openly outrageous in the way they treated their own people. After hearing of the atrocities committed by the Japanese, it was doubly disheartening to me to see the treatment my fellow Chinese were receiving from the troops supposedly there to protect them.

If provincial officials could not raise what they wanted through taxes and rents, they would exact advance payments of taxes for future years from the peasants. Generals would inflate the numbers of their troops in order to get food, money, and matériel for the nonexistent soldiers. When asked to produce these extra troops, the generals would conscript peasants into the army but then not feed or clothe them. With the Japanese closing in from all sides, the victims did not even have a place to run should they want to escape the oppression of their so-called protectors. I was outraged, but I could also see that the generals were simply opportunists, using their power, in the absence of a strong central authority, to line their pockets.

The demoralization that resulted from this corruption ultimately hurt the generals when they tried to rally the people against the Communists. Their failure to control their greed left them without any popular support when they needed it a few years later. Even those peasants who were doubtful about Communism were not about to lift a finger to help their former oppressors. This was poetic justice of a sort because the Nationalists had held back their best troops from the fight with the Japanese in order to prepare for civil war with the Red Army. It would have been in the generals' long-term interest to have behaved ethically even in the absence of a powerful central government.

The routine of work and bombing went on for the next three years. Throughout this period, the Japanese forces were between fifty and a hundred miles away. By late 1944, however, Japan was able to take Kweilin. Just before this, my group was evacuated to Chungking, where I spent the final year of the war. After the Allies crossed the Rhine into Germany in March 1945, it seemed only a matter of time before Japan, too, fell. The American forces had landed on Okinawa, and Japan was in retreat.

While in Kweilin, I had heard about a program to send some of the more highly trained Chinese engineers to the United States. The idea was to prepare them for the reconstruction of China through apprenticeships in American industry. The program was sponsored by the Nationalist government, and it was supported partly by American money. Acceptance was based on a competitive exam. I had learned something about the technology of the United States, at first in high school and college, and then by reading technical articles. Now, suddenly I saw an opportunity to witness American industry firsthand. I promptly took the examination and was accepted into the program. (I placed second in the exam, and my classmate T. L. Wu placed first. Wu also came to the United States for advanced training but later returned to China, where he was persecuted and died during the Cultural Revolution.)

Shanghai, where I had spent so much time, was a cosmopolitan city, attuned to the West. Although I had never traveled outside China, I did know quite a bit about the United States. Though my first love was science and technology, I had also read a good deal about American society. At Chiao Tung, we had used American textbooks. While in college, I had been impressed by a number of American films, including *Gone with the Wind* and some westerns starring Gary Cooper.

Several hundred people were chosen for the program. The group included a few of my college friends from Chiao Tung. We were flown in groups by DC 3 "over the hump," as the route over the Himalayas that linked China and India was then called, on the return flights of planes carrying lend-lease materials to the Nationalists in Chungking. For most of us, it was our first flight, and the circumstances were anything but comfortable. The DC 3—the legendary "Gooney Bird"—has just celebrated its fiftieth birthday. It was and is an incredibly durable plane. There are stories of the plane losing parts of wings, parts of tails, and still flying safely. I flew with ten or so other engineers, and we sat on benches along the side of the plane. This was April 1945, and the Japanese were still active in the area, and so there was some tension during the flight. I never knew whether we had been shot at or not. What I did learn later was that the plane was not pressurized, which made breathing very difficult as we climbed to clear fifteen-thousand-foot peaks.

We landed near Ledo in northeastern India and took a train down to Calcutta, where we waited for about a month for our sea passage to be arranged. I had seen a great deal of poverty and wartime deprivation in China, but things in Calcutta were even worse.

From Calcutta, we traveled by American transport vessel through the Suez Canal. This was only a few weeks after the German surrender, and our ship was one of the first to travel through the canal after it had been cleared. The captain was exceedingly careful for fear of hitting an undetected obstacle or mine. The trip across the Indian Ocean, up the Red Sea, through the Suez Canal, across the Mediterranean, and then across the Atlantic took about a month and brought us finally to Newport News, Virginia, in June 1945.

When I arrived in the United States, I did not have any idea what I would be doing during my two-year visit. But although America was different, it did not present the dangers of the China I had left. It was unlikely that I would be bombed in the United States. I also knew that I would be doing something in a technical field, and science is the same the world over—a language I *could* speak. The fellowship carried with it a hundred-dollar-a-month stipend, which would keep me alive.

When I left for the United States, I knew that I could acquire whatever skills I needed to survive here. I had heard that there was discrimination against Chinese in the United States, but I came here with no insecurities about what I might try to do. By this time, the notion that there were things I could not or should not attempt to accomplish was utterly foreign to me.

2
Harvard

I am never quite able to convince people that I did not suffer culture shock when I arrived in the United States. People insist that I must have been overwhelmed by the things that make America different from China—the wealth, the people, even the food. But this is simply not true. I look for the similarities between cultures, not the differences. When I first came to America, I saw American habits as the product of the country's history, and not as something peculiar or threatening. It was exciting to meet America, but not strange. Frankly the United States seemed a lot like China to me.

Still, from the moment I set foot in the United States until the day six years later when I founded Wang Laboratories, very little happened as I expected. I had come to the United States intending to serve a two-year apprenticeship as a technical observer, and instead I ended up working toward an advanced degree at Harvard. I had intended to return to China after the two years, and instead I stayed in America and made a contribution to the development of modern computers. Retracing the events that led to the founding of Wang Laboratories, I always come back to one remarkable piece of luck. Because of this—and because luck had more than a little to do with my surviving the turmoil in China—I never dismiss luck as a factor in success or failure.

After arriving at Newport News, our group of engineers and scientists went to Georgetown University in Washington, D.C. Because it was summer, there was ample dormitory space for us there until we found a place in a work or study program. And so my first weeks in the United States were spent in a campus setting not totally unlike that of Chiao Tung University in Shanghai. It was a good time to be in Washington. The war was ending, and everybody was in a jubilant mood. I made sight-seeing trips around Washington, but I ignored the monuments in favor of the museums, particularly the Smithsonian.

Although no one in the group had made any arrangements before we left China, the big American companies had been notified about the program, and our group dwindled as various people found apprenticeship positions. In the meantime, the hundred-dollar-a-month stipend was enough to keep the frugal above water. A number of the group went off to work for companies such as Westinghouse and RCA. As I waited with increasing uncertainty as to whether I would find an appropriate position, it suddenly struck me that I might learn more from graduate studies than by apprenticing myself as a technical observer. While no one else had done this, the more I thought about it, the more attractive the idea seemed. We had come here to be exposed to American industrial and technical expertise. How we did this was up to us. Besides, I knew that I could do well in an academic environment.

Unfortunately I was not really prepared to apply to a university. I had not even brought with me a transcript of my academic record at Chiao Tung University. I wrote to Harvard University anyway, requesting an application form for their department of applied physics. A couple of the members of the faculty at Chiao Tung, including the chairman of the electrical engineering department, had studied there. Through them, I knew of Harvard's reputation.

Ordinarily it would have been preposterous for a newly arrived engineer carrying no credentials to apply to Harvard, but luck intervened, and I applied at perhaps the only time in recent memory when Harvard would have considered a case like mine. It was the summer of 1945, and while Germany had already surrendered, Japan did not do so until August 14. In the meantime, most young Americans were still in uniform, and even universities as competitive as Harvard had more openings than they had students.

Chiao Tung University had an international reputation, and my application may have looked good because other graduates had done well at Harvard. It is also possible that the admissions department was familiar with the government program that brought me to the United States. In any event, they accepted me and some of my friends from Chiao Tung who were also in the program and who had decided to follow suit. At least for us, then, getting into Harvard turned out to be easier than finding an apprenticeship in industry!

In September 1945, I moved into Perkins Hall, a Harvard-owned graduate student dormitory next to the Law School. The setting was not entirely alien since, apart from such friends from Chiao Tung as David K. Chung (who had preceded me to Harvard and who later became a chemistry professor at Syracuse University), there were a number of other Chinese connected with Harvard in one capacity or another.

Although I did not speak English particularly well, my written English was adequate. As the years passed, I began to think more and more in English, which solved the problem of continually translating from English to Chinese and back to English again. However, even today, I still think in Chinese at certain times. For instance, I multiply in my head in Chinese. This is partly because I was strongly drilled in multiplication as a youngster, and partly because numbers are expressed by words of one syllable in Chinese, which makes thinking about them quite simple.

In recent years, I have noticed that increasing numbers of Chinese engineers who come to the United States have trouble adjusting to Western scientific notation. I never had this problem because, as I mentioned earlier, I had used American textbooks from high school onward. While it may be easier for Chinese students to study science in their native language, they pay for it later on if they come to the West for advanced training.

I was comfortable at Harvard. If there was any one constant throughout all the changes of my early life, it was that I was always drawn to universities. Since childhood, a laboratory has seemed a second home to me. I also enjoyed the privilege of studying with some of the great minds of the day. Two of my professors—Edward Mills Purcell and Percy W. Bridgman—later won the Nobel prize for work they did at Harvard.

When classes began, I found the work relatively easy, partly because I had spent five years putting my academic training to practical use designing and building radio and communications equipment with scavenged parts. While a student who had come directly to graduate school without practical experience might waste a lot of energy trying to visualize the meaning of problems and the applications of theory, those of us with hands-on experience could get right to the heart of the matter.

I think that any engineer ought to spend a couple of years in the field working on real-life problems between undergraduate and graduate work. Electrical engineering is, after all, an *applied* science, and theory should always be tempered with experience. In two semesters, I satisfied the requirements for a master's degree in applied physics. My first term, my grades were two A+'s and two A's. It put to rest any doubts Harvard might have had about my ability to handle the work.

My alternation between academic learning and practical applications has also affected my approach to solving problems in electronics. My approach is neither purely analytical nor purely practical. I simply think about a problem until a solution suggests itself. Then I try to make that solution work in practice. After my years of scavenging for parts in Kweilin, I automatically try to make efficient use of electrical components. Even when components are abundant and cheap, I still believe that the simplest solution to any engineering problem is the best solution. The fewer the components, the fewer the opportunities for something to go wrong.

Some inventors are born tinkerers who like nothing better than to play with electrical components all day long, and who maintain elaborate workshops at home so they can continue to work late into the night. This is not my style at all. I do most of my serious thinking with a pad of graph paper and a pencil. I am adept at tinkering when the occasion calls for it, but I do not need to have physical objects in my presence in order to work with them. To this day, I do not have a workshop in my home. Nor do I work in thirty-six-hour binges like most "hackers." If I have an idea in the evening, I am content to wait until the next day to see whether it works out in practice. If my first attempt to solve a problem doesn't work, I simply try to understand where I have gone wrong and then make adjustments. The key to doing something right may lie in the feedback you get from doing something wrong. I approach problems in business the same way.

At the time I finished my work for the master's degree in 1946, I still intended to return to China after the second year of the program. My funding, however, dried up after the first year as the Nationalists diverted resources to the civil war with Mao Tsetung. Just as my finances were getting seriously pinched, I got a call from W. K. Chow, a fellow graduate of Chiao Tung, a former graduate student at Harvard, and the man for whom I had worked during the war. Mr. Chow was in charge of a purchasing mission in Canada which bought materials for the Chinese government. I accepted a job with what was called the Chinese Government Supply Agency and moved to Ottawa to start work. My job was mainly clerical: developing specifications for the equipment that the government wanted to order. I went there in November 1946, by which point my funding from the Chinese government had ceased entirely.

From my first day on the job, I realized that I had made a mistake. The work was routine and boring, and given the extreme cold that greeted me in November, I knew I was not going to like the worst of the winter which was yet to come. I quickly decided to try to return to Harvard to obtain my PhD. In December, I wrote to Professor E. Leon Chaffee, who was chairman of the Applied Physics Department at Harvard, asking whether it would be possible to enter the PhD program. I had gotten to know Dr. Chaffee during the previous year at Harvard. I had taken a physics course with him, and because he was chairman of the department, I had had dealings with him from time to time. He was a sympathetic and practical man whom I had grown to like.

Perhaps because I had done well in the master's program, Dr. Chaffee responded promptly and positively to my letter. He accepted me into the program and offered me a teaching fellowship which would pay me a thousand dollars a year in return for ten hours a week as a laboratory instructor. He also agreed to be the faculty advisor for my dissertation. And so by February 1947, I had escaped the tedium and cold of Ottawa. I was back in Cambridge, living in a seven-dollar-a-week boarding house, and taking the obligatory courses for the general examination before I began work on my dissertation.

Even before returning to Cambridge, I vowed that if I was going to get my PhD, I was going to do it quickly. To be honest, I had little choice: with only a thousand dollars to pay my tuition and living expenses, I could just barely scrape by. The situation improved the following September when Dr. Chaffee recommended me for a Benrus Time Fellowship. This stipend allowed me to stop teaching and devote all my time to my PhD program.

Even with the scholarship, I did not have the money to relax my schedule. By May 1947, I had picked a thesis topic—nonlinear mechanics—a project in which I would use nonlinear differential equations to develop a mathematical means of evaluating certain types of electrical systems. The systems I was concerned with involved the simultaneous oscillation of two frequencies and their effects on a mass with nonlinear (read erratic) responses. This was one of the few problems I ever approached without concern for its practical application. The practical purpose it served was enabling me to get a PhD. Still, I attacked it with no less intensity than I would any other problem.

While my thesis may not have had a practical application, the frustrations of dealing with the impact of different frequencies on nonlinear bodies were good preparation for the frustrations of dealing with politics and business—both nonlinear systems in the extreme.

Because of the nature of my business, most people assume that I got my PhD in computer science. Actually it was in applied physics. Indeed, computer science was in its early infancy in the late 1940s, and I do not think that there was a single PhD granted in computer science before 1948.

Even so, at Harvard as well as at other campuses, there was a good deal of activity concerned with the development of computing machines, and after I was awarded my degree, I became a part of that activity. But before that, I really did not have anything to do with these projects, most of which were top secret and dictated by military requirements. While my graduate education had nothing to do with computers, I did take courses in digital electronic circuitry that later turned out to be vital to my computer innovations.

The term *digital electronic circuitry* refers simply to electronic circuits that can have either of two states—on and off. But this simplicity is deceptive. In the 1940s, when such circuits were being developed, there was no consensus as to what would be the best way to develop them. An array of these on-or-off circuits can electronically mimic binary numbers—which are like ordinary numbers except that instead of ten digits, there are only two, 0 and 1. In a binary number, the figure in the "tens" place represents multiples of 2 instead of 10, the figure in the "hundreds" place represents multiples of $4(2^2)$ instead of 100, and so on. For instance: the number 3 would be expressed as 11, 4 as 100, 5 as 101, etc. It sounds unnatural because we are used to thinking about numbers based on our ten fingers, but the shift to a base of two held the promise of bringing the worlds of mathematics and electricity together. If these digital electronic circuits could mimic binary numbers, then, people believed, they might also be arranged to mimic the operations of Boolean algebra (which allows one to manipulate binary numbers the way algebra allows one to manipulate conventional numbers).

When I first studied digital electronic circuitry, research on the subject was motivated by its utility for devices that could perform high-speed computations. Electricity allows such computations to be performed very much faster than any mechanical process. During battle, high-speed computations were essential to control the aiming of artillery pieces in an era of high-speed aircraft and ballistic missiles. Radar—the primary focus of Harvard's research—requires fast computation to convert elapsed time into distance to a target. And toward the end of the war, the search for high-speed computing power gained new impetus from the development of the atomic bomb, which required its developers to perform enormously complex computations.

: While I was working on my PhD, these matters concerned me only insofar as they affected the curriculum at Harvard. At the time, I was more concerned with the situation in China. During dinner and afterward in one of our rooms until late into the night, the other Chinese students and I would discuss the progress of the civil war. Though occasionally someone would hear from family or friends in China, most of our news came from newspapers such as the *New York Times*. Because the news reports were highly biased, I tried to read between the lines, as I had done back in China during the 1930s. Most of the reports spoke of Nationalist triumphs, and yet I knew from fellow students who had received mail from China that the Communists were winning.

Among my Chinese friends, there was a good deal of disagreement about who should win the civil war. There was a large group who were pro-Nationalist, and then there was a very small and very quiet group who were pro-Communist. There were people who said that they would not return if the Communists won, and there were a few students who said that they would not return if the Nationalists won. Between these extremes there were a large number of us who were apolitical but who doubted the ability of the Nationalists to maintain the trust of the Chinese people, and thus their ability to prevail in the civil war.

I was in this group. I had seen the abuses committed by Nationalist leaders, and it seemed unlikely that people who had suffered at their hands would suddenly turn and support them in their fight against the Communists—particularly since Communist troops had earlier fought heroically against the Japanese invasion. While I did not want the Communists to win, I thought that some form of coalition government offered the best hope for China. Otherwise, I saw nothing good coming out of this civil war.

The Chinese Nationalist government had suggested that we return when the program ended, but many of us waited to see what would happen before making up our minds. Of the fifty or so students from mainland China who were in the Cambridge area, I think about half went back to China.

Thirty-five years later, when I returned to China for a visit, I met up with a few of my former fellow graduate students, and they told me what they could of the fates of the students who had returned. A few went on to senior positions in the Communist government, and more than one died later, during the purges of the Cultural Revolution in the 1960s.

By mid-1947, it was fairly clear that the Nationalists were going to lose, and that is when I began to think that I might stay in the United States. The news from China was uniformly bad, once again dominated by reports of massacres. With my parents long since passed away and my younger brothers and sister in the care of other members of the family, there was little for me to return to. I also knew myself well enough to know that I could not thrive under a totalitarian Communist system. I had long been independent, and I wanted to continue to make my own decisions about my life.

Given the burden of my work on my PhD, I did not have the luxury of spending too much time soul-searching. To pass a proficiency exam in French and German, I had to take a quick summer course in French and tried on my own to brush up on German (which I had studied in China). Fortunately proficiency in French and German for someone in applied sciences does not mean the same thing that it does for a student of comparative literature, and I was able to just pass the exam. In the fall of 1947, I took the remaining required courses, and in January 1948, I passed the general examination. That left only the defense of my thesis, which I had completed in December.

Except for the speed with which it was done, I do not count my dissertation as a major achievement. It did not make any fundamental contribution to the body of knowledge in electrical engineering, and it had little to do with any of my later innovations. I had chosen my topic in May of 1947, done some experimentation over the next few months, and then, starting in September 1947, begun to write up my results. I finished writing my thesis in December, submitted it in February, and defended it at the oral exam in the spring. Less than sixteen months after I had returned from Ottawa, I was graduated from Harvard with a PhD in applied physics.

If the substance of my dissertation was not of great consequence for electrical engineering, I quickly became aware that being a PhD from Harvard would have great, positive effects on my career in the United States—a lesson that Americans learn early in life. Instead of being an unknown quantity, and one whose English was at that point still pretty halting, I now had the imprimatur of a PhD from Harvard. This was especially important later, when I founded Wang Laboratories. The technologies I was developing were new, and it made customers feel a little more secure to know that the foreign proprietor of the one-man shop who was seeking their business had an advanced degree from one of the nation's finest universities.

However, a few more things happened before I decided to found Wang Laboratories, three years later. Indeed, it was after receiving my degree that my truly original research at Harvard began. I did this work at the Harvard Computation Laboratory under Howard Aiken, designer of the Mark I, and one of the pioneers of computer development. By accident, I got an opportunity to help make history.

The work I did at the Computation Laboratory also set the stage for the founding of Wang Laboratories. Both of these accomplishments came out of my association with Harvard and Dr. Chaffee, and that association was in turn due to the lucky timing of my arrival in the United States. To be sure, I had to deliver once I was accepted by Harvard, but I suspect that without the

piece of luck that made my application timely, I might never
have had the chance to do so. Thus I never dismiss luck as a
factor in a person's destiny. How foolish it would be for a survivor
of war and anarchy not to believe in luck. In fact, I believe that
it is self-deceptive—even dangerous—to think that one's life is
entirely the product of one's own decisions and actions. The person
who believes that he controls his fate entirely misunderstands the
world and sets himself up for situations in which that misunder-
standing will cost him dearly.

3
Inventing
Memory Cores

When I walked into the Harvard Computation Laboratory in the spring of 1948, I had no idea that my work there would contribute to the development of computers and start me on the path to founding Wang Laboratories. I had a much more practical concern: I needed a job. I had contacted Hughes Aircraft, but when they sent me a pile of forms to fill out for a security check, I decided to walk across campus and see if I could find work at a computation laboratory I had heard about. I did not pursue this possibility because I was eager to work on computers. I did it because the lab was nearby, and I thought I could do the work.

Following interviews with Howard Aiken and Benjamin Moore, I applied for a job as a research fellow at the laboratory and was accepted. A day or so after I started work, on May 18, 1948, Dr. Aiken gave me a problem to solve on the storage of information in a computer. After struggling with the question for about three weeks, the solution presented itself to me. Looking back on it now, the answer seems so obvious that I find it strange that no one had thought of it before—though I must admit that I had an advantage in addressing the problem that Dr. Aiken put before me. As a newcomer, I had not yet accepted the conventional wisdom of the laboratory, and so I was free to speculate in unconventional ways.

When I made my breakthrough, I had no idea of its eventual importance. My project was just one of several going on at the lab. While it was immensely satisfying intellectually, it did not have the aura of destiny. Computer science was a brand-new field at that time. There was only one electronic computer operating in the United States, and it was a huge, cumbersome thing that could do very little compared to modern computers. What we were trying to do was invent the things that would make the computer a usable, general-purpose tool. There was no guarantee that we would succeed.

My invention emerged from the clutter of this era only years later. This is the case with many inventions. The transistor and the laser, both extremely important technologies, were invented during this same period, but it took a number of years for them to begin to have an impact on the world. Those of us working on computers in the late 1940s enjoyed the sense of purpose and the creativity of the times, but I suspect that most of us did not have a sense that we were making history.

The Harvard Computation Laboratory was one of several centers devoted to the development of digital computers in the United States and Great Britain in the 1940s. At other universities, scientists were working on the same questions. Given the egos involved, the period was remarkably devoid of politics. Everything concerning computers was new at the time, and most researchers had not yet begun to specialize—and to jealously guard their specialty. I believe that the open relationships between the labs in the United States and Great Britain, and the absence of government secrecy, sped up the pace of discovery. Perhaps this is why the computer flourished here rather than in Soviet Russia, where there was not nearly as much of this cross-fertilization.

The late 1940s was perhaps the most creative period in the history of computer science. Freed of the secrecy that obscured work during World War II and not yet commercially important to the degree that would make people secretive, researchers speculated openly about what a computer should look like and what it should do.

Virtually every question those of us working in the field came across was fundamental. At the end of World War II, the only computers in the world were electromechanical monsters. These early computers had to be tediously reprogrammed to perform different operations, they had extremely limited memory capacity, and their processing was done by a scattered collection of logic circuits. By 1955, less than ten years later, there were scores of computers in existence, computers which had much the same structure they have today. They could store both data and the programs which determined their operations. The electronic logic circuits had been bunched together into central processing units, or CPUs, which today are the heart of a computer's operations. In fact, the fundamental decisions made back then about the structure of computers still condition computer design today.

A number of people from that era became legends because of their contributions to computer science. The most often mentioned are Alan Turing and John von Neumann. Working independently, they shaped the theoretical design of computers. Even before the first machines were built, Turing described what a computer would have to do to be a computer. And he demonstrated logically that it was possible to construct an all-purpose computer. Von Neumann later contributed the ideas that led to the development of the stored program. Then there were people like John W. Mauchly and J. Presper Eckert, Jr., of the Moore

School of Electrical Engineering at the University of Pennsylvania, who together built ENIAC—the first purely electronic computer. Many of these pioneers came through the lab during the years I was there, although I never got to know any of them beyond a brief introduction and a handshake.

Dr. Aiken was also a pioneer in computer development. He became interested in the field because of the tedious calculations he had had to make in order to finish his doctoral thesis at Harvard in the late 1930s. Aiken designed his first machine to solve relatively complex algebraic equations. This gave him the idea of trying to build a general-purpose machine that could perform different computations depending on the instructions fed into it, a machine that could be programmed, in other words.

This machine, which Aiken and his colleagues finished in 1943, was at first called the Automatic Sequence Controlled Calculator. Later it was nicknamed the Mark I. The machine was gigantic: fifty-one feet long and eight feet high. It virtually filled a room at the Computation Laboratory. With its thousands of mechanical relays, it was so noisy that it was difficult to talk when it was operating. While it was very different from the computers of today, it was still a computer. Moreover, it was the first binary computer built in the United States that was operated by elec- tricity.

A computer, quite simply, is a machine that performs com- putations. A slide rule is a computer. So is an abacus, and so is an adding machine. The slide rule is what is known as an *analog* computer because it transforms numbers into measurements that are in turn manipulated to perform computations. The abacus and other adding machines are examples of *digital* computers. Rather than working with numbers that have been turned into physical measurements of one sort or another, they work with the digits themselves.

As I said before, the great breakthrough that led to the devel- opment of modern computers was the realization that by using a binary system with only two digits, one can mimic all the mathematical operations performed with the ten digits that we are accustomed to. Electrical computations required the use of a binary system: whereas there is no easy way to electrically represent more than two digits, the presence or absence of an electrical charge can be used to represent the two digits—one and zero—of a binary system.

The Mark I that Aiken built was neither purely mechanical nor purely electric, but a combination of the two, "an electromechanical" machine. It created its binary statements through a vast system of telephone relay switches. These switches are quite simple. When a small electromagnet is activated, it pulls two electrical contacts together, allowing current to flow between them. When it is off, a spring pulls the contacts apart and no current flows. Thus, when the current is allowed to flow, the switch can be read as the binary digit one, and when the contacts are apart and no current is flowing, the switch can be said to be in its "zero" state. Using these relays, Aiken and his colleagues created circuits, each of which performed a logical function required to electronically perform arithmetic. They constructed a memory register that could hold numbers until they were needed for operations. They also built a control unit that managed the operations of the computer. They fed instructions into the computer by means of punched paper tape, an idea that dates to the cards designed by Joseph-Marie Jacquard in 1801 to program weaving looms.

While the Mark I was far faster than a mechanical calculating device, it was far slower than a purely electronic one. In a digital computer, the key to speed is how fast the circuit can change state from "one" to "zero." A relay can make this change in about one hundredth of a second. In a vacuum tube, it is possible to make this change in about ten millionths of a second. This meant that if someone could figure out a way to use vacuum tubes rather than relays, it would be possible to speed up operations by a factor of one thousand. Even as the Mark I was being introduced in 1944, Aiken was working on vacuum tube–based, electronic successors to his pioneering first machine.

No matter how fast a machine can perform calculations, its speed is limited by the rate at which it can access the data it needs in order to calculate. In the early days of computing, access to information was a major problem. My own contribution to computer science was to help design a means by which computers could have rapid access to data. This work fell in an area of computer design that was at first called storage and then later came to be known as memory.

Today, when we rank the capacity of computers, we use as a measuring stick how much memory the computer has, and how quickly that memory can be accessed. This habit amounts to a tacit recognition of the importance of memory in the development of computers. Today any person can buy a personal computer with one million bytes of semiconductor memory for just a few thousand dollars. Back in the 1940s, researchers spent millions of dollars to develop computers that only had a few hundred bytes of storage capacity.

Memory has been described as the internal combustion engine of modern computers, and yet its importance has only become evident in retrospect. When I was working at the Computation Lab, many of the things that large-scale memory permitted were only just beginning to be considered. Memory was seen as useful for storing data, but most people then would have ranked computing speed as more important than memory.

On the other hand, once memory became widely available, people in the field began to recognize some of the developments it fostered. For instance, with fast, easily-accessed memory, it became possible to store programs as well as data within the computer itself, making it truly a general-purpose tool. Memory also permitted the development of programming languages and applications which made computers more accessible to nonprofessionals. And memory continues to be essential to future developments in computer technology. If we are one day to be able to address computers in ordinary spoken language, for instance, the machines must have enough memory to perform the operations necessary to translate spoken language into a language that a machine can understand. Today a computer must perform about a hundred million operations to understand a single spoken sentence, which puts a tremendous burden on memory.

Because the basic structure of computers has become somewhat standardized during the last thirty years, we tend to forget that there was nothing inevitable about basic computer design. Even as late as the 1940s there were still a large number of people who believed that analogic computers (the ones that manipulate measurements instead of numbers) rather than digital computers were going to be the machines of the future. Actually this made sense, because analog calculators were faster and cheaper in certain cases if you did not need accuracy beyond two to three decimal places. The first major computer developed in Cambridge was a differential analyzer built by Vannevar Bush of MIT in 1930, and it was an analog machine.

In the late 1940s, the question of memory was unsettled as well. People were not sure what might be the best way to store and retrieve binary numbers. When I began working on the problem of data storage, there were already many types of storage in use or in development. They included: electromechanical relays, vacuum tubes, cathode ray tubes, punched cards, magnetic tape, magnetic drums, and acoustic and mercury delay lines. One computer built by IBM back then used three different types of memory storage at once.

Each of these offered a solution to the problem of storing binary pieces of data, but all had one or more disadvantages. Electromechanical relays were cumbersome, noisy, and slow. Punched cards were stable (data could be stored with the power off), but they were slow. Vacuum tubes were fast and did not require mechanical movement, but they needed a constant source of power and they were prone to burnouts. The delay lines (an ingenious idea that stored data in wave form) seemed promising, but you had to search through every piece of data to find the one you wanted. Finally there were the cathode ray tube memories, which stored information as charged bits of phosphorus on a screen. They were fast—ten times as fast as a delay line—because you could directly address the location on the screen where a particular bit of information was stored, but, like vacuum tubes, cathode ray tubes required a continuous source of power. Still, these tubes were perhaps the earliest form of what is now called random access memory, or RAM.

Of all the various means of storing information, magnetism seemed to hold the most promise then. At the time I went to work at the Computation Laboratory, the problem was that the only method so far devised to store binary information magnetically required cumbersome mechanical means to store and read the information.

This method involved reading magnetically stored information from either a tape or a rotating drum. One magnetic head (like the type you find in a tape recorder) would record the information, while another would read it. The method was simple and involved existing technology. The problem was that both the tape and drum had to be moved to be read, and this made the whole process slow. Even the fastest drums were only a tenth as fast as the mercury delay line, which, as noted earlier, was itself only a tenth as fast as the cathode ray tube.

Thus, the problem Dr. Aiken gave me was simple, but seemingly impossible. He wanted me to find a way to record and read magnetically stored information without mechanical motion. I knew when he gave me the problem that it was possible to read magnetic information without motion, but I did not think it could be done without destroying the information in the process.

The Computation Laboratory consisted of Dr. Aiken, five or six research fellows, and a few assistants. Once I was hired, I went right to work, at first on an ad hoc basis. I was officially appointed a research fellow on July 1, 1948. Each fellow had a great deal of autonomy. In fact, because six people were responsible for designing an entire computer, each of us acted a bit like a miniature R&D department.

The lab itself was a typical electronics laboratory—long on utility and short on design. The building was new back then, made of brick, and it had the institutional look of a public school. The first thing you saw when you walked in the front door and up the stairs was the huge Mark I, now encased in glass to reduce its deafening noise. The upper floor was largely devoted to administrative and operations offices and pine-paneled meeting rooms. Downstairs was a large open space where we had our workbenches. Each of the fellows had a work area cluttered with the paraphernalia of electronics.

Dr. Aiken himself was a formidable and intense man, feared by many of the people who worked at the laboratory. He was tall and sharp featured and had an intimidating stare. He was very strong willed, and unpredictable even to those who had known him for a long time. I remember getting a ride with him on a number of occasions, and he was the kind of driver who had his foot either on the accelerator or on the brake the entire time—he never coasted. He put in extremely long hours, leaving the lab at eight or nine in the evening and returning sometimes as early as four in the morning. I don't think that he ever met anyone—including John von Neumann—who he thought was smarter than he was. He was impatient with small talk, but that was never a problem with me. Because I was still grappling with the language, I tried to be extremely concise when I spoke.

Aiken became something of a legend for impatience with and even cruelty to people he felt were not his intellectual peers, and he was known to publicly berate those unfortunates when he caught them in an error. He had been a Navy officer, and rumor had it that just before the end of the war he had threatened to have one researcher shipped to the front in the Pacific when the man balked at Aiken's order to learn programming. However, if he felt you were his peer, he would rein his temper and even tolerate being contradicted. As a speaker, he was extremely articulate, expressing his thoughts with intimidating precision. He was also an idealist. One of his principal beliefs was that computer research belonged in the public domain, and not to individuals or corporations.

Aiken was a pioneer in computer development, but even he did not see the potential importance of these machines. In 1947, he is reported to have tried to discourage the National Bureau of Standards from backing Eckert and Mauchly by remarking, "There will never be enough problems, enough work for more than one or two of these computers. . . ."

I had very few direct dealings with Dr. Aiken. I rarely saw him as he spent much of his time in administration and I spent all of my time in research. In fact, we met only at regular monthly conferences. I had no firsthand experience of the tirades he was prone to launch into, which I interpret to mean that he accepted me as a peer, and that he was pleased with my work. On the one occasion I did spend a good deal of time with him, he was quite cordial. This was when we traveled together by train to a conference in Washington, D.C. He invited me to dine with him and even went so far as to order a drink for me. At that time I did not drink, and so I was a little worried about the effect alcohol might have on me. However, I gamely put aside my reservations and accepted his offer. There were no catastrophic consequences.

As a researcher, I had a good deal of independence from everyone else in the lab. I appreciated this because I like to work alone and I have always been my own most demanding supervisor. I mostly spoke with Dr. Way Dong Woo, a fellow graduate of

Chiao Tung University, who was also at the laboratory. It was nice to work with someone with whom I could talk in Chinese about technology and events in China. Because I was still a little self-conscious about my spoken English, I did not spend a lot of time in casual chatter with the other fellows.

The computer I worked on was called the Mark IV. It was to be Aiken's first purely electronic computer. Just before I arrived at the laboratory, Aiken and his team had finished designing the Mark III, an electromechanical computer that used magnetic drum memory. (IBM, which funded the Mark I, had become furious with Dr. Aiken when he only referred in passing to the company at the press conference introducing the Mark I. From that point on, they shifted their funding to support computer research at MIT.) The Mark IV was funded by the Air Force, which supported basic research in computers.

As I set to work on the task Dr. Aiken had given me, I faced two entirely different problems. There was the conceptual problem of designing the memory device, and then there was the problem of actually making that design work in practice. As it turned out, I made the conceptual breakthrough within a matter of weeks after my arrival at the laboratory. The practical problem of finding the right materials and implementing my design, however, took a great deal longer.

As I said, I knew when Dr. Aiken gave me the problem of reading magnetic information without mechanical motion that it could be done, with electricity—thanks to a characteristic of magnetism that has been described as a gift of nature to computers: once a material has been magnetized in one direction, it will hold that magnetic direction (called its flux) until it is affected by an electrical current which generates an opposite flux. This meant that you could store information as a magnetic flux of one direction or another, and that information would be retained even when the power in the computer was turned off; the positive flux could be read as the binary digit one, and the negative flux as a binary zero. I could read the information by attempting to magnetize the material in a given direction (for instance, in the negative direction): if the flux was positive to begin with, it would reverse, generating an electrical pulse, and I would read the information as a binary one; if the flux was negative to begin with, it would remain unchanged, generating no electrical pulse, and I would read the information as zero. The only problem was that whenever a flux was reversed, the information it contained would be destroyed. Hence, I too was faced with what seemed to be an impasse.

I had resolved that the best way to store the magnetic information was in a doughnut-shaped configuration called a toroid, because with this shape far less current was needed to create or reverse a continuous magnetic field. I also knew that if I was to be able to read the charge caused by reversing the magnetic field, the magnetic material had to have special magnetic properties. The material would have to have a very strong *residual* magnetic flux, which is to say that the current induced in order to read the information had to be nearly as strong as the original field. Both these pieces of information were common knowledge in applied physics, and they seemed to bring me tantalizingly close to a solution. I tried to think of a way to read the field by applying only a little current, or by using some other method to read it that wouldn't affect its state, but each solution I came up with proved unworkable for one reason or another. At that point, a few weeks into the project, I felt that I had exhausted all possible solutions to the problem.

But then one day while I was walking through Harvard Yard, an idea came to me in a flash. Like everybody else, I had been so preoccupied with preserving the magnetic flux as it was read that I had lost sight of the objective. I realized in that moment that it did not matter whether or not I destroyed the information while reading it. With the information I gained from reading the magnetic memory, I could simply *rewrite* the data immediately afterward. Moreover, since magnetic flux could be changed in a few thousandths of a second, I could do this without any real sacrifice of speed. This concept of rewriting information is the major feature of magnetic core memory.

Thus my solution to the problem was my realization that I had already solved it. With this idea, I had the conceptual basis for a memory storage device that satisfied the criteria that Dr. Aiken had put before me. It was stable, it was fast, and it involved no mechanical motion.

I kept a notebook in which I recorded my progress on the problem. In my notes on June 29, 1948, I wrote, " . . . It is very possible that the information can stay there [in the core in the form of a particular magnetic direction] and be transferred many times before the information [is lost or muddied]. . . ."

What remained now was to find the best magnetic material to use to make the doughnut-shaped "cores" and then to think of a way to link these cores into something that might comprise a computer memory. This was no small task since by themselves the cores could only store individual bits of information.

We searched until we came across a publication from a naval research laboratory which described a soft magnetic material that had been developed by the Germans during World War II. Naval Intelligence had obtained the material, which was called Permanorm 5000-Z, and it was just what we needed. Later Allegheny Ludlum Steel Corporation duplicated the nickel-iron alloy and sold the material under the name Deltamax. It became the basic material of core memory for a couple of years, until it was replaced by materials based on metal composites called ferrites.

To link the cores into a memory system, I took advantage of the fact that the act of reading the information would induce a current. I realized that if I linked the cores in a series, I could use the current generated by one core to read the next core, and so on, until I got to the last core. At that point, I could use the current generated by that core to rewrite the first core. In concept, my application of the cores to memory was essentially similar to the delay lines mentioned earlier. Like a delay line, this arrangement of cores was read serially—it was necessary to pump through the series of cores to get to the particular bit of memory that one wanted. As memory becomes larger and larger, a system like this becomes increasingly cumbersome, and for this reason the application of cores in a delay line never really caught on for mass storage. We used this system in the Mark IV, but not too many other computers ended up using a magnetic core delay line.

Ironically, while this particular application of core memory never caught on, my ideas for the individual cores became the basis of computer memory for the next twenty years. This was because Dr. Jay W. Forrester, working at MIT, heard about the concepts I had developed for devising and reading individual cores, and conceived of a way of organizing these cores into a system that had far greater practical application than a delay line.

Dr. Forrester's idea was to organize a number of cores into a grid, or matrix, as he called it. Each core would be wrapped around the intersection of two wires. If he ran only half the current needed to reverse the magnetic field of a core through any one wire, the only place the current would be strong enough to reverse a field would be at the intersection of two wires. There the sum of the two currents would surpass the amount needed to reverse the magnetic flux of the core. In this way, he could specify exactly which core he wanted to read.

It was a brilliant idea because with this system Forrester did not need to cycle through all the cores to get to a particular bit of information. As with the cathode ray tube memories, he could randomly access the particular memory he wanted. With a system like this, memory size could expand far beyond the few thousand bits permitted by the other high-speed systems then available.

This is exactly what happened. Over the years, people went to work miniaturizing the cores and cramming more and more of them into ever larger matrices. Deltamax cores were big and unwieldy. Ferrite cores were radically smaller. IBM eventually designed a computer with a 250,000-bit core memory. IBM based the 360 family of computers—the workhorse mainframe computer for many years—on core memory and sold over thirty thousand of them during the 1960s. It was only when semiconductor technology began to emerge from laboratories in the late 1960s that magnetic core memory began to diminish in importance. Data processing technicians still refer to a memory dump as a "core dump" in recognition of the role magnetic cores played for so many years. And even today core memory is occasionally used when it is important to retain information despite power loss.

For instance, the space shuttle *Challenger*, which tragically blew up in 1986, had backup computers based on core memory. It was used on the shuttle because it would retain information even in the event of a catastrophe. Investigators looked to the salvaged core memory for clues to the events that led to the disaster.

Clearly it is the idea of the matrix that made core memory such a force in the history of computers, and credit for that idea belongs entirely to Dr. Forrester. What I did was to come up with a well-defined way to read and rewrite a given core. It was a fundamental idea which Dr. Forrester acknowledged, but Dr. Forrester also took the idea a little further.

I can now see that the cores I developed presented opportunities that I did not fully exploit. When you make a breakthrough of one sort or another it is important to try to explore fully the potential of that breakthrough. Having made an unconventional discovery, I should have continued to look beyond convention for further applications of my cores. Had I done so, I might have had the flash of insight that led Dr. Forrester to matrix memory. Instead, we were content to fit this revolutionary idea into the conventional context of the delay line. It was a lesson I took to heart, and never since have I been content to stop exploring the possible applications of an innovation after the first flash of insight.

I have always believed that if I thought long and hard enough about a problem, a solution *might* present itself to me—though, of course, there is no guarantee that I or anyone else can solve every problem. When you immerse yourself completely in a problem, your mind turns back over your training and unconsciously works toward a solution. Usually your first attempt to solve a problem draws upon what you have already learned. But often this is not enough. This is what was happening when I was trying to read the cores without destroying the information. At some point, usually after you have reached an impasse, you are forced to look at possibilities that involve a radical departure from your training—e.g., that it does not matter whether or not you destroy the information so long as it is possible to rewrite it later.

When that insight did come to me, it was in a flash, and not as the logical conclusion of a conscious train of thought. This is the way most of my best ideas have surfaced—presented to me by my subconscious almost as a gift, and not as the product of an arduous struggle. It is not a process I can control or even articulate, and because of this, I am very dubious about the prospects today of creating a computer that might display the intuitive side of human intelligence. I do not know what happens in that moment during which the mind sifts through and then reaches beyond prior learning to find an order that will solve some previously baffling question. For all we know, there may be several different types of intuition, depending on the problem and circumstances. How, then, can we devise a machine to mimic this process? The chances are very slim of making a machine that will do something that we do not yet understand ourselves.

On the other hand, as computer designers become more adept at emulating particular types of reasoning, there is always the possibility that a computer might someday surprise its creator by producing what resembles an intuitive leap. Computers might produce something that resembles human intelligence before we know what human intelligence really is.

Finding a solution to the problem of storage gave me new confidence that I could make a living in my adopted country. Dr. Aiken seemed pleased as well, for he gave me a 23 percent raise after my first year at the Computation Laboratory. This was a big increase, unprecedented in the world of the Computation Laboratory.

I began to work on designing some of the logic circuits for the Mark IV as well. However, by the second year, it became apparent that the days of computer research at Harvard were numbered. Harvard had a policy of not pursuing research in developing technologies once they had matured to the point where they had commercial applications, and by 1950 I could see that this day was not far off.

I was ready to strike out on my own. The real importance of what I had invented would not become apparent for years. I did not know at the time that the invention of core memory would make me wealthy. The intellectual satisfaction of solving what seemed to be an unsolvable problem was its own reward. Once I made this breakthrough, however, I began to turn my attention to how it might solve real-life problems, for me the most satisfying process of all.

II
Some
Calculated
Risks

4
From
Researcher to
Entrepreneur

In recent years, a great many academics have left the security of the campus to start businesses in high technology. However, in 1951, times were very different. It was an era when people believed that what was good for General Motors was good for the country. If a researcher left academia, it would more likely be to join a large corporation than to start his own company. Venture capitalists were not roaming the campuses looking for researchers to back. Indeed, venture capital was all but unknown: the grand-daddy of venture capital in high technology, American Research and Development, would not help found Digital Equipment Corporation (DEC) for another five years.

So my decision to start my own company was considered quite bold at the time. I had come from China only six years earlier, and the field I was entering was brand new. But from my perspective, I was merely taking advantage of an opportunity that appeared to justify rather minimal risks.

However, before I even began thinking about starting a business, I did something that set the stage for that decision. A year and a half before I founded Wang Laboratories, I took the first steps toward patenting my memory cores. It was this move that first started me thinking about commercial applications of my invention.

Also during this transitional period, I became an American—in spirit, if not yet in fact. I was married, and my wife and I settled down to raising a family in the Boston area. I had met Lorraine Chiu in 1948. Although Lorraine was also from Shanghai, her family had long-standing ties to the United States. She is distantly related to Yung Wing, the first Chinese to come to the United States to study at Yale. Wing was graduated in 1854 and went on to an illustrious career on both sides of the Pacific. Lorraine's parents had been born in Hawaii before it was annexed to the United States (and long before it became a state) but had moved back to Shanghai at about the time of Sun Yat-sen's revolution. They were married in China, where Lorraine was born, although she still has a number of relatives in Hawaii. Despite these ties, Lorraine, like myself, found herself very much on her own when the civil war erupted in the late 1940s and cut us off from our homeland.

Although we were from the same city, we had never met prior to our arrival in the United States. To a degree, though, we had had parallel educations. Like me, she had spent her undergraduate days in Shanghai (at St. John's College), and like me, she had continued her studies in the Boston area. She had come to America to study English literature (principally Shakespeare) as a special student at Wellesley, where a sister and friends had also gone.

During those years, the main events in my social life were get-togethers organized for Chinese students and academics in and around Boston. It was at one of these, in 1948, that I met Lorraine. During the next year, we met several more times. We continued to see each other and, in less than a year, decided to marry.

Because of the civil war in China, we could not follow the traditional procedure of seeking her parents' approval of our marriage. Today in the United States, such formalities do not seem particularly important, but for a Chinese couple at that time, not being able to observe the proper forms was no small thing. A year after we first met, in 1949, we were married, and we moved into a reasonably comfortable apartment on Massachusetts Avenue in Cambridge.

M y decision to file for a patent came as something of a shock to my colleagues. I had always been rather quiet around the lab, and so they were surprised to hear that I wanted to do something they regarded as bold. They were also apprehensive about Dr. Aiken's reaction to my decision. They had dealt more frequently with him than I and had experienced his harsh supervision. And knowing his conviction that computer developments should be kept in the public domain, or dedicated to the public, they felt that it was crazy for me to seek a patent for my work on memory cores.

To be perfectly frank, I did not even consider this factor very seriously. I was much more concerned with the relative merits of the decision than I was with the possibility that it might ruffle someone's feathers. By this time, I had had a good deal of experience dealing with stressful circumstances. I was not and am not immune to stress, but then, as today, having made a decision, I did not spend time second-guessing myself or worrying about the consequences.

I recall that I first got the idea of seeking a patent around June 1949, and I discussed it with Lorraine. Lorraine knew a great deal more about Shakespeare than she did about Newton or

Einstein, but she instantly saw the value of patenting my invention. She encouraged me to pursue the idea. Without her urging, I might not have had the courage and drive to seek the patent.

I had heard about other engineers patenting their ideas (though I knew of no one else at the Computation Laboratory who had done so), and my first thought was to see whether Harvard was interested in the patent, or in sharing the rights to the patent with me.

While I had never encountered his wrath, I had heard enough about Aiken to know that I did not want to have any preliminary discussions with him about the issue of patents. Instead, I spoke with people in Harvard administration responsible for managing outside contracts. According to the agreement between Harvard and the Air Force, Harvard only reserved those patent rights that pertained to public health, and the agreement specified that those patents should be filed for the benefit of the public. My invention seemed to have nothing to do with public health (although the management of public health would be impossible today without the help of computers), and the people at Harvard suggested that I file for it myself at my own expense. They did note that since my work was funded by the Air Force, this automatically entitled the United States Government to a nonexclusive license for whatever patents I was awarded.

Because I knew nothing about the ins and outs of applying for a patent, I asked them if they could recommend someone who might assist me. I was told that Harvard was represented in patent work by a lawyer named Edgar H. Kent of the Boston law firm of Fish, Richardson & Neave, and that he might agree to help me.

In September 1949, I went to see Mr. Kent, and I was passed on to a young lawyer, fresh out of law school, named Martin Kirkpatrick. I asked him whether he thought that I had grounds to file a patent for my memory cores. I think that this again was a case in which luck played a role in my life, because this young man was perceptive enough to see the potential of a stable, nonmechanical medium for computer memory. This was no mean feat since, at the time, there were only a few computers in the world, and the field was not well understood at all outside of the research labs. Like many patent lawyers, Marty had done his undergraduate work in science, and he could quickly grasp the concepts involved. This chance meeting also turned out to be the start of a business relationship and friendship that continues today. Within a month, we had prepared and filed a patent for what I called my "pulse transfer controlling devices."

Because my patents ended up being very lucrative, they ultimately attracted challenges and litigation. During the next nine years, until all disputes involving these patents were resolved, I was to have the benefits of an extended tour through the intricacies of patent law.

A patent is fundamental, or broad, to the degree that it does not have to cite other patents and references. Since computer science was a relatively new field, and since my invention was basic, there were almost no other patents to cite. This made my patent a very broad one, as opposed to Forrester's later patent for matrix memory, which had to cite a number of other references, including mine. What this meant was that should I be awarded a patent for memory cores, anyone who wanted to use those cores in any application, including matrix memory (which of course I did not know about at that point), would have to honor my claim.

Any patent or patent application contains a number of *claims* in which the invention is defined in such a way as to distinguish it from prior uses or publications. The same invention will be defined in a number of claims which vary in their degree of breadth—from broad to medium to narrow—and each claim is considered by the Patent Office to be a separate invention. This is so that in case there turns out to be some earlier use or publication which invalidates the broad claim, the inventor is still protected on the intermediate or narrow claims. Neither

Marty Kirkpatrick nor I could envision the ultimate role my memory cores would play in the development of computers, but Marty could readily see that it was a broad patent, and that it had commercial promise.

My patent ended up with thirty-four claims for the structure and uses of memory cores. The most important of these claims was number 24, which reads as follows:

24. A pulse transfer controlling device including a core of magnetic material in which the residual magnetic flux density is a large fraction of the saturation flux density, winding means on said core, current pulse generator means operatively connected to said winding means to apply current pulses of opposite polarity to said winding means, and said pulses of one polarity acting to saturate said core in one direction to read in information, and of the opposite polarity acting to read out said information by inducing voltage in said winding means as controlled by the state of residual magnetic flux density of said core and to reset said core.

This claim describes the basic configurations which underlay all applications of magnetic core memory. As you can see, patent description is not the kind of prose people quote at cocktail parties.

After a patent application is initially filed, there is a process during which the Patent Office judges the clarity and validity of the claims. The Patent Office issues a weekly *Official Gazette*, which contains summaries of all patents issued. If, after reading the *Gazette*, an inventor feels that he had the idea for your invention before you did, he has the right to copy your patent claims in his patent application and petition the patent examiner to declare an *interference*. The patent examiner then decides whether he has the right to begin an interference, and if he does, this initiates a lengthy procedure during which the outcome of the interference is determined. On top of the several years it takes between filing and the issuance of a patent, there might be several more years while interferences are resolved. In the meantime, the inventor has the right to issue licenses to his invention in advance of a patent.

In my case, the process of amendment and refiling went on long after I left the Computation Laboratory, so that when I made the decision to start Wang Laboratories, I was confident, but not certain, that I would have the right to market my invention.

After I filed on October 21, 1949, I braced myself to inform Dr. Aiken of my action. Although I had made my decision, I was still a little nervous about how he would react. It was entirely possible that he would launch into one of his legendary tirades. Ordinarily the cares of the day vanish for me as soon as I get into bed. I recall that the night before our meeting was one of the few times in my life that I had some trouble getting to sleep.

It turned out that my apprehension was groundless. I could hardly say that Dr. Aiken was overjoyed with my news, but he showed no negative reaction. In fact, he did not react at all. Later he gave me another substantial raise, which I took to mean that he was not too put out by my actions. In any event, there was no noticeable difference in our relationship in the year and a half I spent at the lab after our conversation.

However, there were other events after I filed for my patent that caused me to take stock of my situation. By 1950 it was becoming clear that computer technology was developing to the point where companies might begin to produce the machines commercially. Eckert and Mauchly had already formed a computer company, and there were several other commercial projects in various stages of development.

In December 1950, the first Atlas I, a stored program computer developed by Electronic Research Associates, had been sold to the government, and three months later the Census Bureau took delivery of the first UNIVACs developed by Eckert and Mauchly.

As noted, Harvard's policy at that time was not to pursue research in fields that had reached the stage of commercial applications. The feeling behind this policy was that academic resources should be used to extend the horizon of knowledge, and not to develop a better mousetrap. It was not surprising, then, that at about the time the first commercial computers were appearing on the market, those of us who worked at the Computation Laboratory guessed that Harvard was going to de-emphasize basic computer research.

Other universities did not adhere to this policy as strictly as Harvard did. Computer research did not slow down at MIT, for instance, even as the machines moved into commercial production. I feel that Harvard should not have been so quick to abandon basic computer research. Even today there is still a vast amount of computer research that properly lies within the province of universities. In fact, some of that research goes on at Harvard, which subsequently decided to re-emphasize the field. But Harvard has yet to reestablish its earlier eminence in computer development.

It turned out that the Mark IV was the last computer the Computation Laboratory produced during Dr. Aiken's tenure. Work on this machine kept me busy until I actually left the laboratory in 1951. After Aiken finished the Mark IV, Harvard maintained the Computation Laboratory to generate scientific data and tables of various types.

The decision to leave the laboratory was relatively easy: since Harvard was no longer going to sponsor basic computer research, I no longer wanted to stay there. However, I also knew that in leaving I would be turning my back on what had become a comfortable salary—at this point fifty-four hundred dollars a year. I had no real doubts that I would be able to duplicate this salary should I take a job in industry, but I did not want to go to work for a company. I have always treasured independence, and the idea of working for IBM or Hughes Aircraft or Remington Rand or one of the other electronics companies did not appeal to me now any more than it had when I arrived here or when I got my PhD. Nor did I particularly want to look for a position at some other academic research center. What I really wanted to do was try something on my own.

After I filed my patent, I was contacted repeatedly by researchers in industry and academia doing work on computer development. In June of 1949, Way Dong Woo and I had presented a paper on magnetic memory storage at a meeting of the American Physics Society which received a good deal of attention. I had written a couple of other papers for scholarly journals, and these articles had also excited interest in my work. My innovations with memory cores had given me the status of an expert in digital electronics, and with that reputation, I thought I might have the credibility to start my own business.

The more I thought about it, the more reasonable it seemed. I could make and sell memory cores, for which the capital requirements were very small, and I thought I could probably get contracts for special projects in digital electronics.

I measured what I was giving up by leaving the lab against what I thought I might earn working by myself. At risk was my salary of fifty-four hundred dollars, plus my savings of a few hundred dollars (realistically I would have to draw on my savings until I began to receive contracts and payments). On the other hand, I thought that I had a reasonable chance of earning eight thousand dollars or so the first year. Attaining even this modest goal would mean a better than 50 percent increase over my salary.

Thus my expectations were very different from those of many of the start-ups in high technology today. I did not anticipate becoming wealthy. Nor did I have a chart showing steeply curved earnings projections or a business plan. And I did not have the worry of risking somebody else's money.

I did feel that during the next few years there would be a growing need for both memory cores and expertise in digital electronics. And I believed that this would be true whether or not computers revolutionized the way the world did business.

From this perspective, it seemed as if I had a reasonable chance of success. I began to read books about how to run a business, and I asked people how one went about doing such a thing in Massachusetts. I also discussed the idea with my wife. In September of 1950, she had given birth to our first son, Frederick. Fred's birth was followed by complications which forced Lorraine and Fred to return to Boston Lying-In Hospital, where he had been born. The hospital was not prepared for us to return, and so Fred spent his first night back at the hospital in a linen closet! He could not be put back in with the other newborns because he had been exposed to unknown contaminants while outside the nursery. Lorraine later told me that she had been so preoccupied with the baby that the importance of what I was going to do did not dawn on her until later.

This was a big decision, and I did not make it in a day. But as with most of my major decisions since, I did not spend more than a couple of weeks thinking through the pros and cons, and once I had made the decision, rather than worry about whether it was right or wrong, I devoted all my energy to making that decision work.

I discovered that a form of business called a sole proprietorship made the most sense for what I wanted to accomplish. A sole proprietorship is not actually a form of incorporation. At that time, all I had to do to set up a sole proprietorship was go to City Hall and pay a small registration fee, and give my company a name.

In April 1951, I notified the Computation Laboratory that I would be leaving. My one-year contract with them was due to expire in June 1951, so there was nothing unusual about the timing of my decision. Because of the news that the laboratory would be getting out of computer research, a number of other research fellows were leaving as well, and so Dr. Aiken was not unduly surprised. On June 22, I received the papers which certified that I, Dr. An Wang, would be doing business as Wang Laboratories.

In the years since 1951, I have occasionally been asked why I called the company Wang Laboratories, which some people feel makes the company sound like it is in the pharmaceutical business. I could have called it Digital Electronics or Cyberdyne or some other high-tech name. I used my own name in part because at that point my expectations were that I would *be* the company since it was a sole proprietorship, and perhaps in part out of pride. I wanted the company to reflect my values and my origins—and in truth I could not think of a better name. Working at the Computation Laboratory had given me the idea of calling the company Wang Laboratories; while the two laboratories would be very different in scale, I would be doing work at my laboratory that was similar to the work I had done at the Computation Laboratory. I used the plural, *laboratories*, rather than the singular because I thought the company would expand over the years, and I wanted a name that would accommodate growth. I was indeed very naive: I did not think about marketing studies, the reaction of the investment community, or anything else that goes into naming a company these days.

I quickly found very inexpensive office space—at about seventy dollars a month—on Columbus Avenue in the South End of Boston, and I was officially in business. My capital was six hundred dollars in savings, and I had no orders, no contracts, and no office furniture.

My conviction that I was taking a reasonable risk given the potential rewards was not shared by my acquaintances, particularly our Chinese friends. They were sensitive to discrimination against Asians, and they did not think it wise to start a business in an area still perceived to be the province of the establishment. At that time most of the Chinese who had come to the United States for graduate studies chose academia as the arena in which they might prove themselves. To be a full professor at a prestigious university was the summit of success. Lorraine remembers that Professor L. J. Chu, who became a full professor at MIT, was regarded as the most successful member of the Chinese community. Our friends reminded us that the only businesses Chinese-Americans seemed to be involved in provided services of one sort or another. I think many of them expected me to fail.

Once I began Wang Laboratories, Chinese friends called regularly to see how I was doing. When it became clear that I was making a go of it, some of those following my progress decided to try the same thing themselves. Two brothers we knew named Li, both professors at MIT, left academia to found a company soon after I founded mine.

I was certainly aware that at that time there was some discrimination against Chinese, but in the cosmopolitan Cambridge community, my wife and I were somewhat insulated from that discrimination. In the nineteenth century, Chinese had been treated quite badly in the United States, even, on occasion, being attacked by lynch mobs. While things were no longer as violent when I arrived, other, more subtle forms of discrimination persisted. I remember on one occasion we answered an advertisement for an apartment, only to be told when we showed up to inspect it that the apartment was not available. I am convinced that the apartment became unavailable when the superintendent saw that we were Chinese. When I encountered this type of discrimination, my response was to take it as an unpleasant fact of life and then to redouble my efforts to succeed.

Despite the political turmoil of my youth, I have always felt intense pride in the historical depth of Chinese culture. A Chinese can never outgrow his roots. Ancient ideas such as Confucianism are as relevant today as they were twenty-five hundred years ago. There is also a practical genius to Chinese culture that allows it to assimilate new ideas without destroying old ones. As a Chinese, I had also mastered some of the scientific disciplines that have been the special strength of Western societies. In other words, I felt I had succeeded on the West's own terms. Hence I was distressed to see the menial role Americans assigned to Chinese back then, and a small part of the reason I founded Wang Laboratories was to show that Chinese could excel at things other than running laundries and restaurants. Of course, there is no question about that today, but in 1950, things were very different.

However, though the desire to change the image of Chinese in America was a part of my motivation to start my company, it would be a mistake to conclude that I was founding a company to prove anybody wrong; I was founding the company primarily because it seemed like a smart thing to do.

Although I felt my decision was based on prudence, I do not underestimate the role of confidence. My confidence had been built by the risks I had taken in my youth, and now it pushed me to act on my judgment. A number of other researchers may have seen the same opportunities that I did but failed to act. It is necessary to gather facts, and to analyze those facts when considering a course of action, but the world is shaped only by actions, and to take action requires confidence.

Today, thirty-five years after I founded the company, I continually hear people question whether Wang Laboratories can survive the competition with mighty IBM. My response is that the odds against Wang Laboratories surviving in 1951, and then growing to the size it has, were a lot worse than the odds of the company's successfully competing against IBM today.

5
A Modest
Beginning

June 30, 1951, was just an ordinary day as I left our apartment in a red brick townhouse, and drove my pre-war Buick convertible over to 296 Columbus Avenue. There I entered the bare, unfurnished space of about two hundred square feet that was to be the business headquarters of Wang Laboratories.

The first thing I did was to make a capital expenditure of sorts, and purchase a table and a chair. Next I arranged for a telephone. With a telephone and a table and a chair, I was ready to do business. In order to contact people who might be interested in buying Deltamax memory cores, I borrowed a book from the Harvard Library. The book was a directory of government and industry research laboratories, and it listed the addresses and key personnel of all the major facilities in the United States. I methodically began contacting them, either by telephoning or by mailing a flier I had had printed up at a nearby shop. The flier simply announced that I was in business and described my expertise. I had a number of contacts at universities by virtue of my earlier work on cores, and these were the first people I called. A lot of universities and research centers were interested in magnetic cores as a means of storing information, so I expected that I might get orders for cores which they intended to use as samples in experiments.

At the same time, I wrote to the Commerce Department asking for a list of what are called RFPs—requests for proposal. This is a means government agencies use to solicit bidders on contracts of various types. I searched through the lists to see whether there were any projects on which I might want to bid.

And finally I set to work developing ideas that I thought might lead to useful applications of digital electronics. The first project had to do with digital counting devices which could record, store, and display data. At that time, there were really no electrical devices apart from computers that could store and retrieve data, so I figured that I could use my magnetic cores in a number of useful applications. Just as I had kept a notebook at the Computation Laboratory, I kept track of my projects and ideas at Wang Laboratories in a series of looseleaf notebooks. For instance, the entry for July 27, 1951 (only a month after I began the company), contains the reminder: "Make plans to build at least one such unit [a digitalizer and counter] . . . to be demonstrated at next year's IRE Convention Exhibition." As the entry shows, I had adopted the habit, when discussing scientific or business ideas, of writing in English, although at that time I still thought about nonscientific matters in Chinese rather than in English.

I looked forward to trade shows as an opportunity to make contacts and to demonstrate my inventions. In recent years, trade shows have become massive affairs with lavish displays and thousands of participants. Back then, they were much smaller, and a participant might have little more than a desk and a stack of fliers as an exhibit, but they were still the best way to let the electronics world know that you were in business.

If I was going to manufacture cores, I needed the raw material and the tools necessary to do so. Fortunately this was simple. I had already dealt with Allegheny Ludlum Steel in connection with my work at Harvard, and so I had a ready supplier of Deltamax. Making the cores themselves was primarily a process of winding wires around the toroid-shaped Deltamax, and this required nothing more sophisticated than a soldering iron. Later on, I developed a machine that would wind wires around the cores automatically, and this greatly reduced the amount of time it took to make them.

Within three weeks of my first day, I began to get responses to my letters. I was selling the cores at $4 a piece, which is a hefty price considering that one core stored one bit of information. At that price, a 64K semiconductor chip which today sells for about $.75 would have sold for $256,000.

At first, it would be a big day if an order came in for four memory cores. Lorraine remembers that I would come home and say, "We got an order for four cores today!" as though this were particularly good news. In fact, it was.

The first person I hired was a young man studying advertising art at Boston University named Bob Gallo. Apart from doing assembly work on the cores, Bob would hold the fort while I was out of the office. As word got around that I had started a company, a number of business executives and government officials started to come by to visit. Bob, who was young then, was astonished to see generals troop through with their aides. If I was out, he would give them coffee and try to steer the conversation away from technical matters until I returned. He has since remarked that these visitors at first gave him the idea that he was working in something more than a simple electronics laboratory.

I took advantage of Bob's artistic skills and asked him to design a logo for the company. Since I was paying him fifty-five cents an hour, the total cost for the design work on the logo came to less than three dollars, and we used the logo for almost twenty years. Today companies often spend tens if not hundreds of thousands of dollars on research and design work for company logos, so I feel that I got something of a bargain.

During my first month in business, I spent about two hundred dollars of my savings, which left only four hundred dollars. This might have made me nervous were it not for the fact that before the first month was out, orders began to trickle in at a fairly steady rate. A few months after this, I had another piece of good fortune. In 1950, Harvard had started a pension plan. By the time I left the Computation Laboratory, about two thousand dollars had been paid into the plan on my behalf. Not wanting to be saddled with the headache of managing this small amount of money for the next few decades, Harvard suggested that I take the money in a lump sum, an idea I enthusiastically endorsed.

Now, instead of having a cushion of only a few hundred dollars, I had over two thousand dollars. This amount was not that much less than my take-home pay at the Computation Laboratory had been. I was now certain that I could live for a year, long enough to determine whether my company would survive. If it did not, I was reasonably confident that I could find a job.

When I started the company, our son Fred was nine months old. During the next twelve years, we were to have two more children: another son, Courtney, and a daughter, Juliette. During these early years, Lorraine was primarily concerned with the children's education. Chinese families have always stressed academic excellence, and Lorraine closely supervised the children's study habits.

When Fred was old enough to go to school, Lorraine felt that the local public schools were not very good and that we should take on the burden of sending him to private school. This was in 1953, and the eight-hundred-dollar annual fee charged by Shady Hill School in Cambridge—more money than I had when I started Wang Laboratories—severely stretched our budget for the first few years.

While we were concerned with our children's education, we did not try to force any of them in a particular direction. We did not, for instance, push them to study Chinese culture, although, of course, both of us wanted our children to learn the literature and thought of their ancestors. Independence rather than blind obedience was the trait we wanted to encourage in our children, particularly since they would be making their lives in the United States.

At the time Fred was born, Lorraine and I were still Chinese citizens, staying in the United States as resident aliens. Although we planned to stay in the United States, we had not yet become American citizens. In the mid-1950s, however, the People's Republic of China intimated that it was going to demand the repatriation of those Chinese students who had stayed in the United States after the revolution. We were contacted by American government officials, who, in a warmly appreciated gesture, offered us the chance to become American citizens. On April 18, 1955, Lorraine and I became naturalized American citizens. Fred, of course, had been a citizen since his birth.

I was ambivalent about giving up my Chinese citizenship. While I disliked what was going on there politically, China was still my birthplace. Nor did I think that America was a utopia. Indeed, at this time, America was being swept by the irrationality and paranoia of McCarthyism. Still, it seemed to me that America had the best system—as a nation we do not always live up to our ideals, but we have structures that allow us to correct our wrongs by means short of revolution. I am also heartened to see that today both Taiwan and China are hesitantly moving to correct their past wrongs.

I was not the first person to start a company related to computer technology, but in both scale and scope my start-up was very different from most start-ups in high technology. Eckert and

Mauchly founded a company to build commercial computers in 1948, but the vast research and development expenses of their venture forced them to sell to Remington Rand in 1950, before they had even completed work on their first commercial computer, the UNIVAC. A few years after I began Wang Laboratories, Kenneth Olsen started Digital Equipment Corporation with outside financing in order to develop the minicomputer.

Unlike Eckert and Mauchly or Olsen, I had no ambitions at that point to build computers. I probably could not have raised the enormous sums necessary to do so had I wanted to, but more to the point, I did not want to pay the cost of outside financing or to have to be forever justifying my actions to the investors. Not that I wasn't constantly exploring ideas that had to do with digital information processing, but I did so with an eye to whether the ideas could be implemented by a company with our resources at that time.

For example, in setting the price for my first digital counting device, I carefully priced the materials and the labor costs, allowing for a 15 percent rejection rate. I arrived at a figure of $.64 for raw materials. I priced the nineteen minutes of labor necessary for assembly at $.665. I then added factory overhead amounting to $1.15 and a royalty of $.25 to come up with a basic cost of $2.70. Using this base figure, I derived a pricing curve which began with a price of $4 per unit for small volume and decreased to $2.90 for orders of over three thousand units, figuring that my production costs would be halved at huge volumes.

These numbers were a far cry from the millions of dollars in parts and labor which the early computer companies were devoting to developing their machines. But there were other reasons I concentrated on small-scale applications in digital electronics rather than large-scale general-purpose machines. Each of my ideas derived from using digital electronic circuitry to perform some specific function and help solve some specific problem. Consequently I experimented with magnetic memory cores, with shift registers, with logic circuits, and with displays and came up with a variety of applications that would enable people to transform various inputs into electric form and then count or otherwise operate on those electronic pulses. For instance, I devised a tachometer that would read rpms in digital form. I also spent some time thinking about who might benefit from digital counting devices of one sort or another. On the basis of that exercise, I decided to develop a digital counting device that might be suitable for nuclear laboratories, which have to do quite a bit of counting to map the nuclear decay rates of the various elements.

Although I pursued many different types of applications, the fundamental idea behind each application was that digital electronics could make life easier for scientists whose chores involved counting, storing, and computing information. I took the trouble to explore what some of those chores might be and then devised applications that would perform them—in some cases before anybody in the laboratory knew that this was what they needed.

While many of those working with computers were infatuated with enhancing the brute power of their number-crunching machines, I was interested in determining the minimum number of electrical components needed to achieve some particular goal. My business philosophy was not to develop general-purpose machines in the hope that they would prove useful but rather to provide specific solutions, the purpose of which would be self-evident to the user.

I came up with a great number of ideas, many of which were adaptations of my memory cores. A good number never made it from the pages of my notebook to prototype. Still, I remember what a great deal of fun it was to spend my time designing and creating different digital electronic machines. I don't remember fretting about whether or not I would succeed. I would tackle an idea inspired by its immense potential. Most of these projects proved to be impractical, but the chase was fun. The scale of my operation allowed me to make mistakes and pursue false trails without the worry that one mistake or misjudgment would put me out of business. I was prudent, but I was an optimist. I still am.

In December 1951, I had my first opportunity to demonstrate my inventions publicly at a trade show. I piled some Deltamax cores as well as the various digital devices I had developed into my Buick and drove with Bob Gallo to an IRE (Institute for Radio Engineering) exhibition and conference in New York City.

The Wang booth (which consisted of a card table) saw a good deal of traffic during the convention. Bob's job was basically to keep the crowds of visitors happy until they could get a chance to talk with me. He had become adept at that from the hours he had spent entertaining the generals and other officials who had come through the Boston office. I took it as a good sign that my display attracted so much attention. There seemed to be a lot of curiosity about what I was doing. The convention produced a spurt of orders, and I decided to make a point of attending future conventions.

At one of these conventions, I remember running into a fellow entrepreneur, Joe Gerber, the founder of Gerber Scientific Instruments. We congratulated each other on the crowds we were attracting, but we were both worried about whether all this attention would translate into sales.

To supplement my income from the sale of memory cores, I taught a course in electrical engineering at Northeastern University evening school for the princely sum of twelve dollars per lecture. While teaching at Northeastern, I heard about their Cooperative Education Program, in which students divide their time between work and study. As the number of orders for memory cores picked up, I decided to hire a co-op student to work for me part time as well. This man, David Miller, I put to work helping to wind the Deltamax cores with electrical wire.

My finances were precarious that first year. To save money on one occasion, I succumbed to a temptation that ended up costing me what was at that time a substantial amount. Because there was no convenient parking on the street, I used a nearby lot that charged fifty cents a day. After I had parked there for several months, the manager of the lot told me that if I prepaid three months' rent, he would charge me half price. I jumped at the deal. Two weeks later, the man was gone—no doubt staked by a nest egg he had put together from me and a few other innocents. Prior to this, I had not thought that I was susceptible to being suckered in this way, and I took to heart the lesson that deals that look too good to be true or legal probably are not true or legal.

When it came time to tote up my income for taxes in 1952, I was happy to discover that the $3,253.60 I earned from July to December through Wang Laboratories was more than the $2,700 I had received from the Computation Laboratory during the first half of the year. My expenses had been small, the major items being $420 for rent and $298.07 for travel and entertainment (most of which went to pay the expenses of my trip to New York). This was an extremely modest beginning for the company, but by the end of the first year, my cash flow more than covered my operating expenses, and my company was doing sufficiently well to justify continuing for at least another year.

In the fall of 1952, I won a contract to perform research and development services for a company called the Laboratory for Electronics in Cambridge. The contract called for me to develop a pulse synchronizer and counting device. This contract gave me a three-hundred-dollar-a week income, the first steady stream of income I'd had since I founded the company.

As time went by, I began to get more and more consulting contracts to design specialized digital equipment. Many of these projects were subcontracts of government grants of one sort or another. For instance, I received one contract to design a means of automatically recording counts of red and white blood cells. The money for my part of this contract came indirectly from the

National Institutes of Health. Although I designed a device to do the counting, this machine was never completed because a microscope that could actually recognize and count blood cells was still beyond the optical technology of the times and the capabilities of the major contractor.

Despite such false starts, I felt none of the effort was wasted; someday the information gained might prove useful in an entirely different application. I had the opportunity to develop my own solutions to a number of different problems in digital electronics: I had to devise programs that would create numbers on a cathode ray tube (CRT), I had to devise logic circuits to perform various operations, I experimented with various forms of counting, storing, and retrieving numbers, and in all of my experiments, I tried to make the most efficient use of electrical components and ideas.

These projects continually brought to mind the various problems posed by using electronics to perform mathematical operations, some of which would come up again and again during my career. For instance, when I set out to devise an automatic range finder, I was confronted with the problem of multiplication, which was solved by using a method that adds logarithms in order to perform multiplication (the process which is the basis of the slide rule). Ten years later, I used the same method as the basis of the calculator which became Wang Laboratories' first widely distributed product. This approach to adding, which was unique in digital electronics, was suggested by my experimentation during the early years of Wang Laboratories.

While working on consulting projects, I developed a facility with digital electronics that served me well as the company began to develop more ambitious technologies. Although I was very concerned with maintaining cash flow, this time served as an incubation period during which I learned about both the marketplace of digital electronics and the essentials of running a business. I was concerned with innovation, but only insofar as innovation served the needs of the marketplace. This approach to technology and the marketplace has characterized my company ever since.

The patience and moderation that characterized my start in business paid off in many ways. Even during the early years, the business grew at a good rate, but the growth started from such a small base that I could easily learn what I needed to know in order to manage the company at its next stage. Each year, I increased my base of knowledge about business and the marketplace, and although I made mistakes from time to time, the mistakes were small, like the company, and not a threat to its future. If there was a threat to the modest and well-ordered way in which I began my business, it came not from a mistake or failure but from the fact that my memory cores ultimately attracted the attention of one of the most powerful companies in the country, IBM. Out of a correspondence grew a relationship that was to continue in various forms until this day.

6
First
Encounters
with IBM

There is one thing that the heads of all the computer companies in the world—no matter how large or small—have in common. We have to deal with IBM, either as the company that already dominates our market, or as the Goliath that might at any moment enter it. It is not a prospect that any CEO takes lightly.

If I have had any advantage over other CEOs when it comes to dealing with this fifty-billion-dollar company, it is because our relationship dates back thirty-five years, to the days before IBM entered the commercial computer business. Indeed, my invention of magnetic memory cores played a role in IBM's entrance into the commercial computer market. The negotiations that enabled IBM to use my invention were like a very high-stakes game of poker. This early encounter gave me a look into the way IBM works, which served me well in later years as the growth of Wang Laboratories brought me ever closer to competing with this giant.

Even before I founded Wang Laboratories, I had written to IBM to see whether they might be interested in buying a license to my pending patent on magnetic memory cores. In June of 1951, I received a reply from a Mr. J. A. Little, the director of market research at IBM, saying, among other things, that they would have to see my patent application before they could decide. I sent them the original patent application, and we began a correspondence. In fact, I began receiving letters from various IBM officials, some of which indicated that different divisions of IBM did not know that I had already sent them the patent application. Nearly a year later, for instance, I got a letter from H. F. Martin requesting information on static magnetic memory. By now, however, it seemed more probable than ever that magnetic cores arranged in matrix form were going to be the near-term solution to the problem of mass storage.

Although I was unaware of it at the time, IBM already had a number of people working on the development of core memory in matrix form. Later it became evident that they had a much deeper interest in the subject than a casual form letter would indicate. Furthermore, I was likely to be awarded a fundamental patent pertaining to this type of information storage, and Marty Kirkpatrick was not so sure that I should give IBM the details of my invention without an agreement that gave me some protection—or rather, let them know that they (or *someone* at IBM) already had the information they sought—and neither was I.

This did not discourage IBM, however, and in July I received a visit from H. R. Keith. Keith was later to become head of IBM's Service Bureau, which IBM was forced to turn over to Control Data Corporation after the settlement in 1956 of Control Data's antitrust suit against IBM, but at that time, he reported to James W. Birkenstock, who functioned as a trusted lieutenant and troubleshooter for Thomas Watson, Jr., the company president. (Birkenstock, who seemed to be the principal figure in IBM's attempts to buy or license computer patents, was ultimately to take over IBM's negotiations with me.) Keith was among the first of the many IBM executives who would visit Wang Laboratories—and discover, no doubt to their surprise, that it was a one-man operation housed in what might be called a tenement. During the year to come, he was also the first to bring up the issue of IBM's licensing my invention. And on December 24, 1952, the IBM patent department wrote to me asking me to send them information pertaining to three additional claims I had filed in my amended application. Again, on Marty's advice, I declined. We had not yet come to any agreement, and I did not want to show them all my cards.

A year after the first discussions of a license, Marty Kirkpatrick and I proposed an arrangement whereby I would do some consulting work for IBM. The idea was that I would devise a way to utilize my magnetic cores to perform some memory functions for an IBM electronic calculating device—the 604—that relied upon punched cards and vacuum tubes for storage of information. At one point in the negotiations, the suggestion was made that my royalty payment for the license be one penny per bit of memory storage. Unfortunately this was never put in writing. In time, the royalties would have amounted to many millions of dollars.

After dickering for some months about the terms of this proposal, IBM and I finally came to an agreement on November 16, 1953. I agreed both to consult for IBM and to grant them a three-year option to buy a nonexclusive license for cores and core circuits as defined in my patent applications.

The consulting arrangement guaranteed me a minimum of a thousand dollars a month income for the duration of the option. This was a considerable amount of money in those days, and by itself, the arrangement gave my young company financial stability while only occupying me for about a week out of every month. I fulfilled the terms of my contract to develop a magnetic-core-based calculator, filing reports and keeping track of the time I devoted to the project. However, I do not think that IBM was actually interested in this project. I believe that their real concern was the option on my patent and, secondarily, having access to my thinking about the different applications of magnetic cores. This impression was borne out by a letter from Mr. Keith requesting my patent application and pertinent documents "as soon as possible." It was also borne out by visits from technical people at IBM, who would come up to my offices, ask about a particular application of the cores, and then leave, only to return a month or two later and ask about the viability of some other application of the cores.

I was surprised by IBM's slowness to grasp the wide range of applications of a stable magnetic storage medium. Even Mr. Keith commented to me on this once. I would have thought that a company with the resources of IBM would have very quickly moved far ahead of me in exploring these uses. Instead, they moved in an almost plodding way, leading me to think that the company was technologically conservative. It occurred to me then that this characteristic slowness might create opportunities to compete against the company in due course despite its huge size.

At the same time that IBM was sending their technical consultants to see me, they were also devoting considerable resources to adapting Dr. Forrester's invention of matrix memory. It was this work, which was taking place both at IBM and at MIT, which had intensified IBM's interest in my patent.

In July 1952, Dr. Forrester and his associates had chosen IBM to manufacture the digital computing equipment for an air defense computer they were developing. The project was called SAGE, and it represented a giant commitment of resources. By November 1953, when I finally signed our agreement, IBM already had three hundred people assigned to its part of Project SAGE.

Dr. Forrester's idea of developing a random access matrix memory dated back to 1949. Bill Papian, one of Forrester's associates, had visited me a number of times at the Computation Laboratory to learn about the principles of my memory cores. By combining the idea of the matrix with my idea of the magnetic memory core, Papian, Forrester, and IBM scientists began to rapidly expand the internal memory of computers. In 1951, the largest array could hold just a few hundred bits of data. By 1953, MIT began testing a computer that relied upon a thirty-two-by-thirty-two-by-seventeen array of ferrite cores for its main memory. The array gave the computer 17,408 bits of memory, and in August the MIT group replaced the Williams tube memory (a form of electrostatic storage) in the Whirlwind I computer with this ferrite core array. With each increase in the scope of matrix memory, my pending patent on magnetic memory cores became ever more valuable.

Eagerness to expand the boundaries of technology was not the only thing that prompted IBM's participation in Project SAGE, and in mid-1954, IBM was sufficiently confident that ferrite cores would provide a workable memory to begin assigning people to work on the development of core memory for commercial computers.

I was not aware of all this activity at the time. But as IBM moved toward commercial production of computers with ferrite core memories in 1955, the question of whether or not they would exercise their option to license my invention became a major issue. The cautious and probing way in which IBM approached me suggested that they devoted a good deal of energy to determining which patents would govern the commercial use of magnetic storage, and who would ultimately prevail in those patents that were disputed.

For instance, Forrester, who had filed an application for his patent for matrix memory in May of 1951, found himself in a protracted interference battle with Jan Rajchman of RCA, who had filed for an application with similar claims on September 30, 1950. Since my patent application was filed earlier and its claims were broader and thus dominated any patent of Forrester's with regard to magnetic storage, IBM was intensely interested in what patent claims I would be awarded, and whether these patent claims would be challenged by some third party.

Between 1952 and 1955, Marty Kirkpatrick and I had been amending my application in response to various demands from the Patent Office. For instance, because a publication issuing from the Moore School of Electrical Engineering about its EDVAC computer project referred to the possibilities of magnetic storage (without specifying how it might be accomplished), the Patent Office added a reference to this publication in June 1953. This was the only reference to pertinent prior art in my patent application, but this unexpected discovery surprised us, and we had to amend a couple of broader claims. In January 1955, the Patent Office allowed thirty-four of my claims, and in April, Marty was informed that I would be issued Patent Number 2,708,722, including thirty-four claims pertaining to my invention, on May 17, 1955.

Just before this, there began a complex series of events which exposed me to the full brunt of IBM's ability to intimidate during negotiations. I am sure that much of what my lawyers and I perceived as attempts at intimidation IBM would argue was merely the exercise of due diligence in determining the worth of the property they sought to buy. Nonetheless, timing and bluff played an important role in our negotiations, and they were affected at the eleventh hour by an event totally unanticipated by me or my lawyers, and which to this day I remain convinced was instigated by IBM.

In early May 1955, when it was certain I would be awarded thirty-four claims on my patent application, Mr. Keith wrote to

Marty Kirkpatrick, saying that IBM would like to discuss the question of exercising their option to license my patent. A key consideration governing these negotiations was the fact that there is a period of one year after a patent has been issued during which the Patent Office, at the request of a third party, can declare an interference. This meant that we both would be negotiating while uncertain about whether or not an interference would be declared. This constraint put pressure on IBM, who by now had a very large commitment to magnetic memory storage, to come to an agreement with me before the year was up. Even if there was an interference, I would almost certainly retain a number of my claims, and if there was not, by May 17, 1956 (the deadline for an interference to be declared), I would be in a position to virtually dictate terms to IBM. On the other hand, the year waiting period gave IBM the opportunity to raise the spectre of potential inter-ferences—and the huge legal costs entailed in fighting the bat-tle—in order to create a sense of insecurity in my camp.

However, questions about potential interferences did not come up at first. Our initial negotiations centered on the question of royalties. The first casualty of these talks was the agreement Marty and I had hacked out with IBM over many months in 1952 and 1953. IBM flatly stated that, given the numbers of cores that would be involved in the commercial production of computers, the original royalty rate would become too burdensome to IBM.

IBM's decision to abandon the terms of the original agreement caused us to consider the idea of selling the patent elsewhere. Fish, Richardson & Neave contacted Research Corporation, a company formed by a number of universities to commercialize their inventions and return a percentage of the royalties to the universities in the form of grants. We quickly discovered that this was not an attractive option because Research Corporation insisted on retaining a substantial percentage of the benefits of any patent they took over and managed. Given this, it looked as though we would have to work out some sort of arrangement with IBM.

Over the summer of 1955, we tried to negotiate either a royalty schedule or outright purchase of the patent. At one point, Marty Kirkpatrick and I proposed that IBM buy the patent for $2.5 million. Mr. Keith replied that "even half of $2.5 million is too high."

In the early fall, the climate of the negotiations subtly began to change. On October 3, Mr. Kent of Fish, Richardson & Neave received a letter from Mr. Keith which outlined a proposal to purchase my patent for $500,000 plus 70 percent of all royalties accruing from the licensing of the cores to third parties. The proposal had grown out of a meeting between the two groups the previous week, and I was ready to agree to these terms. However, added to the proposal were a number of clauses which Mr. Keith said were "designed to afford IBM some measure of protection in the event the patent is successfully attacked by a third party." These clauses stipulated that I warrant the date of my conception; that I warrant the validity of the patent; if an interference was declared, that I accept a moratorium on payments until its issue was determined; and in the event the patent was successfully attacked, that I return up to 40 percent of the money I had collected at that point.

I felt that these terms were unacceptable, and we were again at an impasse. This was resolved by the idea that, together with IBM, we would conduct an investigation to uncover any potential threats to the patent. There was nothing unusual about this proposal. Indeed, it was the type of thing that I would have done were I in IBM's position.

At that point, IBM raised three main concerns: that EDVAC might be construed to have prior art with respect to some of my claims, that Dr. Aiken might claim that the invention was his idea, and that Way Dong Woo might claim that he should share credit for the invention. I was not particularly concerned about any of these fears. While those working on EDVAC had thought about the possibility of using changes in magnetic flux as a means of storing information, they had published no information about how this might be achieved. There was nothing in any of their publications disclosing the read-in of information plus the destructive read-out and rewrite that was the basis of my invention. I also knew that the conception that lay behind the patent was mine alone.

IBM's fears about Drs. Woo and Aiken revolved around the fact that they had both been senior to me when the Computation Laboratory was working on the Mark IV, and that Dr. Woo and I had coauthored a paper on magnetic storage. Moreover, Dr. Aiken was well known for his feeling that all patents coming out of academic computer research should be dedicated to the public, and both Mr. Kent and the people at IBM thought that there was a possibility that Dr. Aiken would suddenly decide to challenge my patent in order to keep it in the public domain.

During the investigation, Marty Kirkpatrick took affidavits from a number of my colleagues at the Computation Laboratory, but he failed to interview either Dr. Woo, who was too ill to speak with anyone at the time, or Dr. Aiken, who simply refused to be interviewed. As I expected, the affidavits by my colleagues contained no suggestion that the invention was anything other than mine alone. IBM also commissioned another law firm to study the vulnerability of my patent from the point of view of a challenge from the designers of EDVAC.

While all this was going on, IBM came up with a list of fifty-eight questions which they presented to Mr. Kent. I first saw this list in mid-November 1955. The questions attacked my patent application from what seemed to be every conceivable angle. The document even raised doubts about the date of my disclosure of the patent—June 12, 1948. Someone at IBM had taken the trouble to determine that June 12 had been a Saturday, and they assumed that the Computation Laboratory had been closed on weekends. It was not.

A good number of the questions were irrelevant (such as when I learned of the existence of Permanorm 5000-Z, the material I settled on for the cores), others (such as whether Aiken had attended a particular seminar) I could not answer. However, most of the questions either I could answer directly or Marty could answer with the help of the affidavits he had collected from my colleagues. Although the purpose of the list of questions was purportedly to reassure IBM, given that I had rejected the clauses in their proposed agreement, I felt the list of questions relayed the message that it is possible to raise doubts about a patent no matter how invulnerable its owner considers his position to be.

After Marty and I had faithfully responded to the questions, it seemed to me that there might be no further impediments to concluding an agreement, particularly since at that time I thought—erroneously, as it turned out—that IBM's option expired in February of 1956.

Once again, IBM had some surprises in store for us. In early January, they pointed out a forgotten clause in our agreement that gave them four months after the expiration of the option to come to an agreement to buy the patent. Simultaneously we were informed that despite this clause, IBM was willing to come to an immediate agreement. Shortly after this, in a conversation between Mr. Kent and Mr. A. Robert Noll, IBM's chief patent attorney, IBM revealed its thunderbolt. The following passages are from a letter Mr. Kent wrote to Mr. Birkenstock on January 18, 1956:

> . . . By mutual agreement, investigation was undertaken jointly to see whether questions IBM was raising, and which led to its requests for warranties, might not be resolved. As

far as we are concerned, that investigation has been completed. However, we understand that IBM still wishes to interview Dr. Woo and that IBM has also uncovered a third party's pending application, which it believes will certainly lead to an interference. . . . Mr. Noll is not at liberty to inform us of the facts regarding this potential interference.

We learned that this "third party" was an inventor by the name of Frederick W. Viehe, a public works inspector for the city of Los Angeles. None of us had ever heard of him before, but we soon learned that he had a number of patents in his name, and that he had been involved in interference battles with a number of large companies, including General Electric and AMF.

This revelation was a shock to me and my lawyers, whose attention had been focused on the issues raised in IBM's list of questions. Moreover, given this new information, it was difficult to understand IBM's actions in the following weeks. For months IBM had been stalling, holding back, ostensibly because of its fears about the vulnerability of my patent. Now, with their discovery of a patent application which in their judgment would almost certainly lead to an interference, they suddenly wanted to move immediately to an agreement with me. Why? Later events suggested that IBM knew more about Mr. Viehe's patent application than they were telling us at that time.

If the patent had been my only asset, I might have been willing to spend the rest of my life protecting it, but this was not the case. The negotiations with IBM had been very time-consuming, and they had distracted me from the rest of my business. My research agreement with IBM expired along with its option in February, and I was eager to turn my attention to new projects. Should I hold out for better terms from IBM, I would be faced with the prospect of several more years of negotiations, either with IBM or with some other company.

Moreover, I had no idea what was in Mr. Viehe's patent application, and so I had no idea how serious his challenge might be. I also had no idea *when* this mysterious challenge might occur. The deadline for requesting an interference was May 16 of that year, but it might happen anytime before then.

If I failed to come to terms with IBM, I might well have to fight an interference with my own resources, which at that time were not great. Given IBM's behavior so far, there was also the possibility that if I did not come to an agreement with them, I would end up fighting the interference with IBM in the opposite corner, using the resources and aggressiveness that they had given me a glimpse of during our negotiations.

Of course, I might emerge from an interference battle in an even stronger position than I was in at the moment, given the importance of magnetic cores and the virtual certainty that I would win some of my claims, but that moment might be several exhausting years away.

On the other hand, if I accepted IBM's offer, I would still emerge with $500,000, which in 1956 was a great deal of money, and the financial burden of fighting an interference, should one be declared, would shift to IBM.

In light of these considerations, I decided that it would be in my best interests, and in my company's best interests, to reach an agreement with IBM even if that meant compromising on some of the issues which I had earlier found objectionable. I would have liked to get the most out of the patent that I could, but if I ended up with 20 percent less, life would still go on, and I would have other ideas to occupy my attention.

After our initial shock at IBM's revelations, everything proceeded swiftly and smoothly. By March 2, 1956, we had a draft agreement. The agreement specified a payment schedule for the $500,000, and eight conditions under which the final $100,000 would be withheld. I signed the agreement, and on March 6, 1956, I assigned Patent Number 2,708,722 to IBM. At this time, IBM, with over $300 million a year revenues, was ten thousand times the size of Wang Laboratories.

One of the conditions I had agreed to under which IBM could withhold payment of the final hundred thousand dollars read as follows: "5a: The declaration of interference involving the patent or any of its claims." This event happened on May 2, 1956, exactly two weeks before the deadline for an interference to be requested. Marty Kirkpatrick received a notification from the patent examiner that my patent had been adjudged to interfere with Frederick Viehe's patent application for an electronic relay circuit that had originally been filed on May 29, 1947. The notification specified that sixteen of my thirty-four claims were involved in the interference.

The usual interference involves the question of who conceived of an invention first. This one was different. There was no question that Mr. Viehe had made his invention first, having filed his patent application a year before I had even begun to work at the Computation Laboratory. Rather, the issue was whether Mr. Viehe's application disclosed the invention defined in my claims. And at first, this was not an easy thing to determine. Mr. Viehe's application ran 550 pages and contained 250 claims.

Because Fish, Richardson & Neave had done so much of the work on my patent, IBM, whose responsibility it now was to defend my patent, retained them to work on the interference. It went on for a year and a half before it was finally decided, and it involved hundreds of pages of documents.

I will not go into the particulars of the interference here because it was highly technical. To phrase it in patent attorney language, the issue was whether Viehe's electrical relay circuits could be construed to encompass a device which uses changes in magnetic flux to read in, read out, and subsequently rewrite a core, as set forth in my claims.

At first, the Patent Office held in favor of Viehe on five of the sixteen counts (claims are called counts in interference proceedings). While this still left my patent with a substantial number of claims, I wanted to pursue the matter because I felt that there was no basis for Viehe to win on *any* of the counts. Ultimately we were allowed a final hearing before the Board of Patent Interferences, which is the last forum for appeal in the Patent Office (it is possible to appeal to the federal courts beyond this point).

However, after this final hearing, while we were awaiting the decision of the Board of Patent Interferences, something happened that raised doubts in my mind about both the interference and the motives of IBM. In November 1957, we received notice that Viehe had assigned to IBM all right and title to his patent application. In the first place, the news that IBM had bought Viehe's patent caused havoc for us because it meant that now, at the eleventh hour, the case had become IBM versus IBM. Thus, we had to make a case that the board should even proceed to a final determination. Because all testimony had been taken and the only thing remaining was the board's decision, they decided to render a decision based on the "merits of the issues raised and the arguments presented at the final hearing."

On December 29, 1959, the board held in my favor on all except one count, the fifteenth, which they awarded to Viehe. This count went to Viehe principally because, in the particular invention to which this count referred, I had not specified the purpose of a rectifier. In the board's view, without this specificity, my claim fell within the broad description of the electrical connection in Viehe's claim. I would have argued this point as well, but because IBM now owned both patents, there was no way to do so. In fact, I believe that IBM only went this far out of fear of antitrust problems.

Thus, we emerged from the interference with the patent almost entirely intact. For me, however, the fact that IBM had purchased Viehe's patent application immediately raised a host of new questions. When did IBM first see Viehe's patent application, and what was their relationship with Viehe during the final months of my negotiations to sell my patent? (This is important because no third party can see a patent application unless an interference is declared.) Where did Viehe get the idea to challenge my patent?

Because the hundred thousand dollars I had forfeited was at issue, my suspicions were not trivial. However, I was advised by Marty Kirkpatrick and Charles Goodhue, an associate and later a partner at the law firm of Goodwin, Procter & Hoar, that the costs of an attempt to prove that IBM had somehow been involved in Viehe's decision to challenge my patent would be considerable and that the chances of success were remote. When confronted on the issue, IBM maintained, as they did when they had first raised the issue, that they had met with Viehe's lawyer, Reed Lawlor (they would never tell us when), and they had discussed the patent application, but that Lawlor had refused to show it to them.

IBM is reputed to have paid Viehe a million dollars for his patent application. Viehe died at the age of forty-eight in 1960, before his patent was issued on January 31, 1961. He died after being stranded in the desert during a rock collecting expedition. A UPI account of his death took note of the fact that the public works inspector left an estate of $625,000. Part of the account reads as follows: "An attorney for Mrs. Viehe, T. Gregg Evans, said Viehe made his fortune through sale of a secret invention. But he was sworn to secrecy regarding the invention and sale."

"'The invention was sold outright,' said Evans. 'The person who bought it got Mr. and Mrs. Viehe to agree never to divulge anything about it.'"

Viehe's son later identified IBM as the party that bought the invention. This pall of secrecy aggravated my suspicions. Fifteen years later, one of Viehe's lawyers still refused to discuss the matter when interviewed by a reporter from *Datamation*. He told the reporter, David Gardner, that they had been sworn never to reveal even the name of the purchaser. Since IBM had made no such demands of me during our negotiations, Viehe's secrecy left the impression that the circumstances of the sale would be embarrassing to the purchaser: IBM.

My belief is that IBM came to the conclusion that buying both our patents might be cheaper than buying one of them should one patent emerge as dominant, and they used each of our patents to induce insecurity in the other camp in order to drive down the price.

Years later, David Gardner, the *Datamation* reporter, brought to my attention a memo that emerged during a legal struggle over matrix memory. The memo was written by the late J. William Hinkley, of the Research Corporation, and it recounted various meetings that involved Thomas Watson, Jr., and James Birkenstock of IBM, among other people. Hinkley writes, "Sometime during a discussion among Birkenstock, Julius Stratton [then president of MIT], and Thomas Watson, Jr., Birkenstock commented that they had probably underpaid Wang or Viehe for their patents . . . in view of the tremendous increase in the size of the computer industry. Birkenstock apparently put this forward as an example of how good a negotiator he was, but was severely taken to task by Watson."

Although it would have been nice to receive a price reflecting the true value of my patent to IBM, in the end, I feel that I had more important things to do than to spend all my time and energy fighting legal battles. Whether four hundred thousand dollars was 80 percent or 8 percent of what the patent was really worth, in 1956, it had the effect of making me well off overnight. At that time, my annual income from Wang Laboratories was about ten thousand dollars a year.

The energy that I might have expended feuding with IBM over price I put into developing new ideas and new directions for my company. To have become obsessed with the patent would in effect have carried with it the suggestion that my most worthwhile ideas were in the past, and I did not feel that this was the case at all.

More than one company has found itself crippled because the CEO became obsessed with a particular injustice or project. I was more eager to get to work on new projects than I was to fight a court battle to prove that I was right and IBM was wrong. Nor could I ignore the fact that the money from IBM gave my company financial stability at a very vulnerable period in its history.

I seriously doubt that after IBM bought the patent, anyone there thought that they would encounter me or Wang Laboratories again. After all, I now had enough money for a comfortable life, and my company could continue to explore niches of the digital electronics market. If I had said to IBM back then that tiny Wang Laboratories would one day be directly competing against IBM's greatest strength, they would have justifiably thought that I had gone mad. I never made this prediction, but this is exactly what has happened.

The sale of the patent was my first encounter with IBM's no-holds-barred style of competition. In the coming years, there would be other, more frequent encounters, and to my mind, the company has not noticeably mellowed in its tactics. But with every passing year, Wang Laboratories has been in a better position to fight these battles on more equal terms.

7
Misalliances

My attitude toward mistakes in business is somewhat similar to my attitude toward failed experiments in technology. Both are inevitable and provide valuable feedback that can direct you to the right path. You have to risk failure to move forward. What is important is to be adaptable enough and diverse enough so that no single mistake will jeopardize the future.

This lesson was driven home by two experiences in the years following the sale of the patent to IBM. During those years, Wang Laboratories gradually changed from a proprietorship whose primary business was consulting in digital electronics, into a company that developed and sold its *own* products. As a consulting company, we did not need a sales force, a large-scale manufacturing operation, or a service division. But later, as we moved into marketing our own products, we had to add all of these functions and more.

This transition was not without its missteps. One led to a temporary alliance with another company which carried with it a sobering penalty. I gave up control of 25 percent of my company's stock, though not control of my company. Shortly after this, I became involved with another company in order to develop a phototypesetting system. This device, called Linasec, proved very successful, so successful that our partner decided to make and market the machine itself. Although in some ways both experiences could be attributed to bad luck, in retrospect, I believe that a couple of my own decisions at a critical point in my company's growth taught me lessons that helped me manage the company better than any lesson learned at business school.

In the late 1950s, to compensate for the end of my consulting arrangement with IBM, I vigorously pursued government contracts. While these contracts provided a steady flow of income, they were frustrating in many other respects. One of the high points of working to turn an idea into a practical piece of equipment is seeing that equipment at work solving everyday problems. Quite often I would devote considerable time and energy to successfully satisfying a government contract, only to have my developments disappear without a trace to some forgotten corner of the bureaucracy.

Apart from being frustrating, this tendency of the government to file and forget about projects also deprived me of feedback, which is essential to the process of innovation. One wants to hear about how a device performs or fails to perform, and about how the user is affected. Thus, I began to feel that being too dependent on government contracts would be not only frustrating but unhealthy if my company was to have the necessary discipline to compete in the marketplace. On the other hand, in the course of working on some of these government projects, I came up with an idea that later became the seed of Wang Laboratories' first product.

In 1954, I first began to think about the problem of translating angular measurements into electronic pulses that a digital computer could understand. While it might seem that I picked a terribly obscure problem to attack, I knew that solving this problem was necessary to a host of different applications I was thinking about. In 1954, I was interested in developing a digital navigational tool for pilots. Although this project did not get off the ground, I did figure out a way to allocate a blip on a CRT to each point on the compass—in other words, a way to translate angular measurements into digital electronic impulses.

A few years later, I was awarded an Air Force contract to help to devise a digital means by which airports might measure the cloud ceiling. To achieve this, I turned again to the problem of digitally encoding angular measurements. I built what I called an angular encoder. This time, I was helped by a technological breakthrough in electronics that had finally reached the point of commercial applications: the transistor.

The transistor enabled those of us working in digital electronics to begin to cram electrical components into modules which could in turn be linked together on a printed circuit board. For instance, we could construct boards which performed basic logical functions. These *logic cards*, as they were called, were the forerunners of today's semiconductor chips. At the time, the biggest company in this business was the Computer Control Corporation. DEC, which was then only a couple of years old, also manufactured the boards. And so did Wang Laboratories. While working on the government's cloud-ceiling-measurement contract, I had gotten the idea that companies might like to buy the separate boards containing individual logic functions. With these boards, they could put together their own packages of digital electronics, customized to perform various functions. I called the boards

Logiblocs, and sold them through contacts I had made in the course of my consulting work.

During the latter half of the 1950s, there was feverish activity as transistors began to have an enormous effect on the digital electronics industry. The transistor opened up vast new areas where digital electronics might improve productivity. It occurred to me, for instance, that the angular encoder I had invented might be used to automate machine tools such as lathes, milling machines, and grinders. If I could figure out a way to electronically control the operations of this kind of equipment, the productivity gains would be enormous.

I envisioned a system that would automatically operate the tools according to whatever instructions might be fed into the control unit by a program of some sort—for example, punched cards, paper tape, or magnetic tape. This would allow operators to vary the tasks of a machine with virtually no downtime, since the machine would do whatever the program told it to. Moreover, given the speed of digital electronic computation, my proposed control system would be much faster than other control systems during any particular operation. I did much of the work devising the components for this system myself. Although I did not realize it then, I was designing a primitive precursor to an industrial robot.

Our customers for this automated control system were machine-tool makers and companies using machine tools. We also sold components separately if a company wanted to build their own automated controls. In fact, we sold the various types of control units under the brand name Weditrol, which stood for Wang Electronic Digital Control Units. They cost about seven hundred dollars apiece at the time, and I recall that we were making and selling between sixty and eighty units a year during 1958 and 1959.

Later, we found new applications for the components we had devised for the machine tool control units. I used one device as part of a package to drive one of the first digitally programmed scoreboards at New York's Shea Stadium. We adapted another component to monitor power lines for Duquesne Light and Power. The system was battery operated, and when there was a power failure, it was designed to print out the sequence of events as the sectors went dark. During the famous blackout of 1965 that darkened much of the Northeast, this battery-operated monitoring device helped the power company to reconstruct what had happened.

During this period, a number of things happened that put a strain on company finances. In 1958, I used some of the money I had received from IBM to purchase land along Route 128 in Reading, Massachusetts. At this point, Wang Laboratories, which had moved to Cambridge in 1954, was employing ten people, and I was looking for space to expand. However, after I had purchased the land and a good deal of building materials, the Commonwealth took the area under eminent domain in order to widen Route 128. I found a temporary solution to the situation by leasing six thousand square feet of space in an office park in Natick, another suburb of Boston. While eventually I got back the sixty thousand dollars I had invested in the land along 128, for a time, I found my finances stretched because we still had to find larger permanent quarters for my expanded staff.

For the short term, this problem was alleviated by a loan arrangement with the First National Bank of Boston. Peter Brooke, who is now a well-known venture capitalist, was then an officer of the bank. He had been asked to help involve the bank in high technology. Apparently he had compiled a list of research-based companies in the Boston area, and Wang Laboratories was on the list. Brooke came to see me and offered me a better deal than I was getting at New England Merchants National Bank at the time, the major feature of which was that I would no longer have to personally guarantee loans.

This credit line temporarily took care of any short-term cash flow problems, but it did not permit me to recruit the administrative, sales, and engineering people I needed to maintain the momentum of growth. Consequently lack of access to credit once again loomed as a threat to the company's future. It was at this point that the idea of an alliance with a larger company was first proposed.

Three years earlier, in 1955, I had incorporated the company. Back then, even though I had not yet concluded an agreement with IBM, it had still been likely that the patent would bring me a substantial amount of money. Since Wang Laboratories was a sole proprietorship, I was personally liable for the debts of the company, and this would have placed at risk any money I gained from the patent. So Marty put me in touch with Charles Goodhue, and Mr. Goodhue began to work on the problem of incorporation.

In the midst of the negotiations with IBM, on June 30, 1955, Wang Laboratories officially became a corporation. I was the president and treasurer, and myself, my wife, Lorraine, and Marty Kirkpatrick comprised the first board of directors. At that point, the company's assets consisted of twenty-five thousand dollars, and its balance sheet was a single handwritten piece of notebook paper. Its original stock issue consisted of fifteen thousand shares of preferred stock, a fifteen-thousand-dollar debenture, and a hundred shares of common stock, all held by me. However, I very quickly reduced the amount of my holdings by giving stock to my wife and family.

An associate of Chuck Goodhue, Bill Pechilis, pointed out to me a clause in the estate laws that allowed you to pass on to your children a sixty-thousand-dollar lifetime gift without paying a gift tax. I asked Bill to draw up the papers to establish the Wang Family Trust for the benefit of my children. We established the trust with Marty Kirkpatrick as trustee, and on April 5, 1957, I gave to the trust a fifteen-thousand-dollar par debenture dated July 1, 1955. This is the only asset I ever gave the trust, but the timing of the transfer turned out to be very favorable. The debenture converted into common stock in later years, and with the growth of the company, it has appreciated enormously.

Today, although the Family Trust is some fifty thousand times larger than it was at its outset, Marty is still the trustee. Bill Pechilis still advises me on tax matters, and were Chuck Goodhue still alive, I would continue to rely on his advice as well. I consider myself fortunate to have met these three men so early in the life of my company.

This, then, was my situation as I began to consider an alliance: Wang Laboratories was incorporated, and apart from the debenture I had given to the Family Trust, the only other person who owned stock in the company was my wife, Lorraine.

One of our customers for machine tool control systems was a Cleveland-based machine tool company called Warner & Swasey Company, which at that time did about fifty-six million dollars a year in business. While First National Bank did not want to go beyond the credit they had already extended to me, Brooke suggested that I might raise additional funds through a debt and equity relationship with a larger company.

In recent years, there has been a vogue for such relationships between large and small companies. Today, Wang Laboratories has a number of alliances with small start-up companies. The logic behind such arrangements is that the larger company benefits from the entrepreneurial energy and innovation of the smaller company, while the smaller company gets much-needed cash and exposure to the management and marketing expertise of a larger company without giving up control of its own destiny.

This was the sort of alliance Peter Brooke and I discussed. Warner & Swasey seemed like a natural candidate for such a relationship. As a major customer for my machine tool control units, Warner & Swasey would obviously benefit from the ideas I had about automating their equipment, and Wang Laboratories would benefit from an infusion of funds as well as exposure to the business methods of a large established company.

Peter Brooke basically acted as broker to this alliance, mediating between myself and Dr. James C. Hodge, who was executive vice-president of Warner & Swasey. After doing some calculating, I had worked out that we needed $150,000 over the next year and a half to cover our expansion needs. In the fall of 1959, we worked out an agreement, the essence of which went as follows: Warner & Swasey would make available $150,000. Fifty thousand dollars of the sum would be an equity investment, for which they would receive shares equivalent to 25 percent of Wang Laboratories. The remaining $100,000 would be available in the form of loans which I could make at a rate .25 percent over the prime rate. Warner & Swasey would also have the right to a seat on the board of directors of Wang Laboratories and favorable treatment with regard to any of our patents, as well as a look at the books of the company.

This was straightforward enough, and certainly I had no complaints about the way in which Dr. Hodge acted as a director of Wang Laboratories. In fact, Dr. Hodge remained on our board until his death in 1982, long after he retired from Warner & Swasey in 1970.

After I concluded the deal, however, I mentioned it to Malcolm Viar, who had been my accountant for several years. He told me flat out that I had made a mistake, that I had sold 25 percent of the company for too little, and that I had given myself the handicap of minority controls. It turned out that Malcolm was right.

Despite my respect for Dr. Hodge, I regretted the alliance almost at once. In the first place, I had enough money from the sale of my patent to IBM and did not need the investment from Warner & Swasey. While it is prudent to keep private and business funds separate, I think that were it not for the fact that some of the money from the patent was tied up in the land that had been taken by eminent domain, I might well have financed the expansion myself or found some other way, without giving up 25 percent of the company. I was to discover that selling stock when a company is young and small and private is an expensive way to raise funds. I had resisted doing this in 1951, but I succumbed to it in 1959. It was a mistake, and a lesson.

Secondly, the alliance never really made sense strategically. Although I was given an inside look at a larger company, what I saw was bureaucracy and internal strife. Moreover, the company was in a declining industry beset with all the problems of smokestack America. I saw very little about the way Warner & Swasey did business that I wanted to emulate. Also, Warner & Swasey was in the machine tool business, and while machine tool controls were a substantial part of our business, I did not see this as the future of Wang Laboratories. This point was later brought home to me by Dr. Hodge, who knew the machine tool business well enough to advise me to stay away from it. Unfortunately this advice came too late.

Finally, there were ramifications to the agreement that I did not really understand at the time of signing which became more onerous as Wang Laboratories grew larger. For instance, the agreement contained restrictions on the issuance of stock which, had they not been amended, might have prevented Wang Laboratories from going public. Warner & Swasey consented to amend our agreement, since at the time we went public, it was very much in their financial interest for us to do so.

From Warner & Swasey's point of view, the agreement must have seemed a tremendous success, especially since, I think, they initially expected that their investment in Wang Laboratories would prove to be a tax loss. While they might have been disappointed that they did not benefit as much from my expertise in digital electronics as they might have wanted to (I do not like to travel and only visited their Cleveland operation a few times), they could be nothing but delighted with the appreciation of their 25 percent stake in Wang Laboratories. Warner & Swasey made a hundred million dollars on their fifty-thousand-dollar investment. Indeed, the stock appreciated so much that the company found it in its financial interests to donate some of the stock to a charitable foundation.

The alliance with Warner & Swasey caused problems for me and Wang Laboratories far in excess of any benefits that I derived from using their money rather than my own. But the mistake was not so much in entering into the relationship as it was in allowing events to get to the point where I felt that the alliance was a necessary step to take. Looking back, I think I had probably been overreaching, and had to pay the penalty of negotiating from a vulnerable and exposed position.

Still, some good did come out of the Warner & Swasey relationship. The capital and loans I obtained from them enabled me to develop the phototypesetting device called Linasec. While Linasec turned out to be a very successful product, it, too, taught me a lesson: that one should be wary of building a product that another company will market, since the other company might get the idea of building the product itself.

In the late 1950s, phototypesetting was still a relatively new field. Most newspaper printing was done mechanically through what was called hot metal type casting. The major problems of typesetting involve editing and proofreading on the one hand, and justification (the arrangement of text into columns of a particular width) on the other. This was before the days of word processing, of course, and editing and proofreading were done on hard copy, and for the most part by hand rather than by computer. However, justification, which primarily involves character and space counting, seemed to be well suited to automation by computer. In fact, even in the late 1950s, there were phototypesetters that would allow one to justify text using a CRT, but these systems were extremely expensive, costing upwards of a million dollars.

The major problem with phototypesetters was their inability to hyphenate words too long to fit at the end of a line but which, if removed, would leave a line too short. Thus, there was an enormous opportunity for someone who could automate the hyphenation process, and thereby increase the productivity of a newspaper.

IBM was one of the companies attempting to penetrate this potentially lucrative market. Their original solution to the problem was to store something like a hyphenating dictionary in the typesetting computer so that if the computer came to a line which required that a word be broken, it could search the dictionary to find the correct response. This worked, but because computer memory was still so expensive, it was a little like using a howitzer to kill a fly.

Another company that tried to profit from this challenge was called Compugraphic. Compugraphic was a Cambridge-based firm that had been founded in the mid-1950s by a couple of entrepreneurs who had defected from another phototypesetting company. Like many other high technology companies of that day and this, Compugraphic was born in a garage. Their start-up was a harbinger of the defect-and-start-up cycle that became a craze in Silicon Valley two decades later.

Compugraphic had been keeping its eye on Wang Laboratories. One day, the president, William Garth, approached me with the proposal that Wang Laboratories design and build to their specifications a phototypesetting machine which they would then market. The idea strongly appealed to me. Designing and building a machine like this was just the type of hardware challenge I enjoyed. Compugraphic maintained, at the time, that they were not interested in manufacturing the machine themselves, and that they would not be a competitor.

Despite such attractions, this was still a formidable project for a company our size. It involved financing, designing, and building a machine with no guarantee of success. In this case, our relationship with Warner & Swasey was a positive factor. The infusion of funds I had received from them made it possible to take on the project without jeopardizing the financial security of the company.

Compugraphic also had a sensible solution to the problem of hyphenation. Instead of loading the system with the hardware and memory necessary to make computer decisions about hyphenation, they suggested that I design the system so that when the problem of breaking a word arose, the system would simply stop and signal the operator. The operator could then look at the screen and make the appropriate decision, following which the computer would resume justifying the text.

Using this approach, Wang Laboratories was able to design, patent, and manufacture a semiautomated justifying typesetter that was vastly cheaper than the competing fully automated systems. We devoted three man-years of engineering work to the project—a big commitment for an organization of about twenty people. But with this commitment of resources, we were able to develop the machine in less than a year. We called the finished machine Linasec, and we received about thirty thousand dollars (depending on what peripherals went with it) for each machine Compugraphic sold.

Because Linasec was so much cheaper than competing equipment, Compugraphic sold a great number of them. The market consisted primarily of small newspaper publishers. In fiscal year 1963, the first year we manufactured the machines in volume, we booked about $300,000 in orders for Linasec; in 1964, about $470,000; and in 1965, about $640,000. With sales of Linasec soaring, Wang Laboratories' sales exceeded $1,000,000 for the first time in fiscal year 1964, thirteen years after I had founded the company. This might seem like a long time to get to

$1,000,000 in sales, but given that Wang Laboratories had started with sales of under $10,000, it represented a rather steep rate of growth.

The future looked very promising. But before I had time to really savor this success, I received a startling piece of news from Compugraphic: they had decided to manufacture Linasec themselves. Even though Wang Laboratories owned the patent on Linasec, Compugraphic had retained the right to manufacture the machines without paying a royalty. Because we had developed the machine under contract to Compugraphic, we had never attempted to market the machine under the Wang logo. At that point, we didn't have the people to market Linasec anyway. Thus we were helpless to do anything about the Compugraphic decision.

The news came as a blow. By the time they told us of their decision, we had manufactured about seventy of the machines, which had brought in better than two million dollars in revenue. We were also projecting about a million dollars in additional revenue from Linasec in the near-term future. Suddenly any revenue predictions based on sales of Linasec looked very shaky. We were about to lose two-thirds of our next year's projected revenue. I vowed at that time never again to design and manufacture a product for another company to market.

Still, I have few regrets about Linasec. It was the most challenging technological project we had yet undertaken, and the success of the machine was rewarding in and of itself.

I have similar feelings about my alliance with Warner & Swasey. Even though I learned some hard lessons from the episode, there were benefits, too. The capital and loans I obtained from them enabled me to do the development work not only on Linasec but also on a new desk-top calculator that marked a key point in the growth of Wang Laboratories. From this point on, I was able to finance growth through ordinary borrowing. I never again had to enter into a similar relationship. While I felt that the alliance was a mistake, it was hardly fatal, and its importance to my company was more in the nature of a lesson than a serious threat to Wang Laboratories' independence or future.

There is a somewhat ironic twist to the end of my relationship with Warner & Swasey. In the mid-1970s, Warner & Swasey still owned about 6 percent of Wang Laboratories' stock. They were carrying that stock on their books at cost, and I had warned them repeatedly that with a hidden asset worth scores of millions of dollars, they would prove to be a tempting target to some predatory conglomerate. I alerted them to these dangers because, should they be acquired, their large block of stock could well pose a danger to Wang Laboratories: the owner of that block had the right to force us to into a registration for a public offering should they want to dispose of their holdings.

At that time a man named William Agee was president of Bendix. Before Agee met his match in his famous struggle with Martin Marietta, he was a very aggressive acquirer of companies. It was at this time that he came across Warner & Swasey. Agee looked at Warner & Swasey and discovered that block of Wang stock carried at cost. He also realized that he could pay for the acquisition of Warner & Swasey through the subsequent sale of that stock.

This is precisely what he did. Once Warner & Swasey discovered that Bendix was on their trail, they came to me and asked whether Wang Laboratories might be interested in playing the role of the white knight and purchasing the company. I declined; I knew the company and its problems too well to want another alliance with them, and I had already learned my lesson.

My father, Yin-Lu-Wang.

My mother, Z. W. Chien, and aunt, Z. T. Chien, in the 1920s.

生以諱女
時初三光緒
生九年二
日二十
丑月一

二十世諱德翰後至二十三世世系表

鳴時
字崑崧
別號景虞
邑庠生
同治龍
傳隱孫

初十五年貢生
正月初十日
同治九年
貢生歷國
時九月七日
亥年五
卒葬

傳勳
字景龍
別號隱孫
高等學堂畢業
盧氏郵傳部
二十
妻氏錦上
十八日卯時生

遷皖婺源汪氏宗譜
卷二
世系表
究

傳猷
後嗣
鳴泰

家均

家祺
亥月十
時初八民國
生八年二
日四二

家慶
亥月初十民國
時初五年
日四二

家平
二十字
日七國
亥月十
生月

家均
後嗣傳
民國猷

家安
字
寅二年民國
十十二
生時九
日月八

山阿墅圖二
週文主鄉一荒
冶誦上
清海庚
女沈向
子日九同氏配甲新
次女女子日月二
裕二四丑女二十
長殤時十年光緒
星一生八四
海時初年
錢生二十
氏娶上卯
錦日八

縣名二申月
李珍名時十四
炳適女生三年
生吳一子穴圩

My childhood home in Kun San,
thirty miles from Shanghai.

*The scenic hill from which nearby
Kun San derives its name.*

*The canals that crisscross the
center of Kun San.*

My sister Hsu Wang, twenty-one, and I, twenty.

The library building at Chiao
Tung University in Shanghai.

A photograph taken at the time of my graduation from Chiao Tung University.

Professor E. Leon Chaffee, my early mentor in physics at Harvard in whose honor I endowed a graduate scholarship.

A new student at Harvard.

Courtesy of the Division of Applied Sciences, Harvard University

The Mark IV, one of the world's first computers.

*Professor Howard Aiken, head of
the Computation Lab and
computer pioneer.*

Courtesy of the Division of Applied Sciences, Harvard University

At work in the Computation Lab.

An early magnetic delay line incorporating my research on memory cores.

A recent photograph of the site in
Boston which was the first office
of Wang Laboratories.

The first logo of Wang
Laboratories.

*Lorraine and I on our wedding
day, July 10, 1949.*

INTERNATIONAL BUSINESS MACHINES CORPORATION

WORLD HEADQUARTERS: 590 MADISON AVENUE, NEW YORK 22, N.Y., TELEPHONE PLAZA 3-1900

August 1, 1951

Dr. An Wang
1 Dana Street
Cambridge, Massachusetts

Dear Dr. Wang:

  Supplementing my letter of July 24th to you,
I am writing you further to obtain a general idea as to what
arrangements you have in mind to interest us in the pulse
transfer controlling devices and methods which we presently
have under study.

  It is also noted you indicated that you are now
self-employed, and we wonder whether you have given consideration to becoming affiliated with our organization.

  Any information that you can furnish us along the
above lines will be very much appreciated, and will provide
a basis for discussing the matter further in person with
you later, as you have suggested.

Very truly yours,

J. A. Little,
Director of Market Research

EMH/h

*An early letter from IBM
indicating interest in memory
cores.*

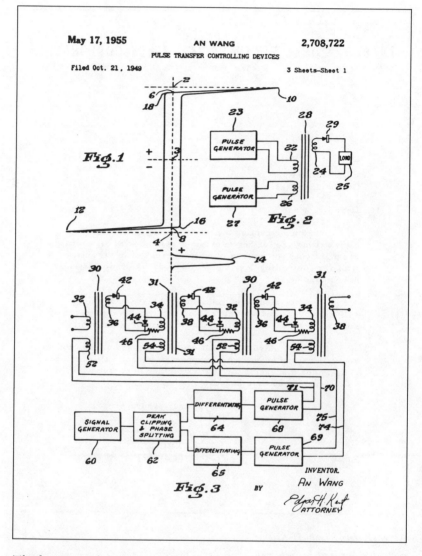

May 17, 1955   AN WANG   2,708,722

PULSE TRANSFER CONTROLLING DEVICES

Filed Oct. 21, 1949   3 Sheets—Sheet 1

INVENTOR.
AN WANG
BY
ATTORNEY

The front page of the patent for "Pulse Transfer Controlling Devices."

Wang Laboratories, Inc.
Opening Entry – June 30, 1955

100	Cash	2566 54		
102	Petty Cash	100 00		
104	Accounts Receivable (see Page 2)	2724 05		
106	Inventories	996 50		
150	Electronic Equipment	1761 91		
152	Machinery	939 40		
154	Furniture and Fixtures	1065 66		
156	Special Tools	313 50		
108	Prepaid Items	664 81		
151	Reserve for Depr.- Electric Equip.		1294 69	
153	Reserve for Depr. – Mach'y + Equip.		52 446	
155	Reserve for Depr. – Furniture + Fix.		248 51	
157	Reserve for Depr.–Special Tools		78 38	
201	Accounts Payable (see Page 3)		2622 68	
202	Accrued Items (see Page 4)		1263 65	
300	Preferred Stock		15000 00	
250	Debentures		15000 00	
301	Common Stock		100 00	
		36132 37	36132 37	
	To record transfer of the above			
	assets and liabilities from the proprietorship			
	to the corporation.			
	Supported by schedules on the			
	following pages.			

The balance sheet of Wang
Laboratories on the date of its
incorporation.

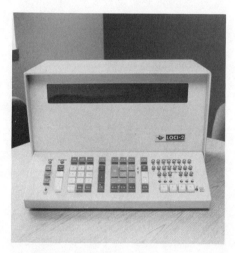

The LOCI desk-top calculator,
introduced in 1965.

The 300 series desk-top
calculator, introduced in 1965.

NEW ISSUE

240,000 Shares

Wang Laboratories, Inc.

Common Stock
(50¢ Par Value)

•

Price $12.50 per Share

White, Weld & Co.   **Tucker, Anthony & R. L. Day**

Kidder, Peabody & Co.   **Smith, Barney & Cc**
Incorporated   Incorporated

Bear, Stearns & Co.   **Clark, Dodge & Co.**   **Estabrook & Co.**   **Hayden, Ston**
Incorporated   Incorporated

Burgess & Leith

August 24, 1967

═ Stock Talk ═

Wang Comes on With a Bang

By DONALD WHITE

And here come's Tewksbury's Wang Laboratories, Inc., to join the list of exciting new issues.

Traded for the first time Wednesday, Wang stock ended the day at 40½ bid after opening at 35 bid, 38 asked.

The offering price was $12.50. Quite a one-day performance.

Wang, manufacturer of electronic desktop calculators and computers, will use the proceeds of the 240,000-share offering to repay short term bank loans, expand marketing operations at home and overseas and enlarge production facilities by about 10,000 square feet.

The company was organized in 1965 by Dr. An Wang. He and his family retain about 64 percent of the outstanding common stock. Thus, on the basis of Wednesday's trading, they have a paper fortune of more than $45 million.

In the fiscal year ending June 30, Wang had sales of $6.9 million and net earnings of $784,599. This is equal to 50 cents a share and means Wang stock is selling at a price/earnings ratio of around 80.

Here's the sales breakdown for 1967:

—Calculators, 62 percent, or $4,259,000. Feature of these solid-state desktop devices is that the keyboard is separated from the electronics package to permit modular expansion into a complete system. Price range, $1690 to $5130.

—Desk top computers, 17 percent, or $1,180,000. Principal item is the LOCI (Logarithmic Computing Instrument) designed primarily for scientific, engineering and statistical operations. Price: $2750 to $8450.

—Digital devices and instruments, 10 percent, or $710,000. These include a punched tape block reader used in tape-programmed production, testing and manufacturing equipment.

—Digital systems, 11 percent or $751,000. A line of transistorized digital logic modules which perform measurements of voltage, frequency or angular positional data. Prices: $3000 to $50,000.

Backlog is currently more than $2 million.

The company employs 400 at Tewksbury, including 24 in professional engineering capacities.

*The announcement for the initial public offering of Wang
Laboratories stock and a* Boston Globe *article recounting the
success of the first day of trading.*

The cover of an industry publication showing me with the company's newest product, the 700 calculator for engineering applications.

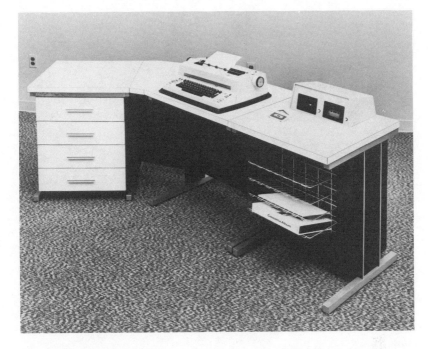

The 1200 Word Processing System, introduced in 1971.

The WPS, one of the earliest easy-to-use, screen-based word processing systems, introduced in 1976.

Fred Wang (right) on his wedding day with his brother and best man, Courtney.

Juliette Wang.

Lorraine and I.

The Wang Center for the Performing Arts.

The Wang Institute of Graduate Studies.

Wang's corporate headquarters in Lowell, Massachusetts.

*Internationally respected China
scholars Dr. C. Martin Wilbur
(left) and Dr. John K. Fairbank
(right), both members of the
Wang Institute's Chinese Studies
Advisory Committee.*

III
Growth
and Control

8
Entering the
Marketplace

I am not the type of person to brood. Although Compugraphic's decision to market its own Linasec machine was a blow, I quickly turned my attention to minimizing its effects. Fortunately we had a product in the pipeline that looked like it could make up for the loss of Linasec sales. We had used the Warner & Swasey capital and loans to develop a product called LOCI, an acronym for logarithmic calculating instrument. Despite its formidable name, it was really nothing more than a desk-top calculator. Long before the term *user-friendly* became a buzzword in the computer industry, this calculator embodied the concept of a machine that is designed with the user in mind. Today desk-top calculators have disappeared, having been replaced by pocket calculators. But in 1965, when Wang Laboratories introduced LOCI, they were a great novelty.

In the early 1960s, if you wanted to perform any calculation more sophisticated than addition or subtraction, you basically had to use a mainframe computer. A mainframe could perform multiplication by a high-speed series of additions. Similarly the great speed and capacity of the mainframe permitted designers to break other higher operations down into repetitions of simpler operations without paying any real penalty in performance. At that time, no one had quite figured out how to perform these calculations in ways that might require less computing power and less memory. There were some other desk-top calculators available, manufactured by companies such as Olivetti, Victor, Monroe, and Friden, but the more sophisticated the problem, the more cumbersome these machines were to use. Scientists quite often have to deal with things like the eighth root of a number, and on one of the other early electronic calculators, solving a problem like this was a terribly slow process.

LOCI, which fit on a desk top and whose sixty-five-hundred-dollar base cost was but a tiny fraction of the price of a mainframe, could add, subtract, multiply, divide, compute roots, and generate exponential values with the stroke of a few keys.

The basis of LOCI had been a tool of engineers and scientists for centuries—logarithms. A logarithm is an exponent of a number. For instance, the logarithm of a thousand to the base ten is three. What this means is that the number ten (the base) has to be raised to the third power (the exponent) to produce the number one thousand. If you want to multiply two numbers, one way to do so is to add their logarithms. Thus, if you can generate the logarithm of a number you can reduce the problem of multiplication to one of simple addition. Similarly, if you want to divide, you can subtract the respective logarithms. Exponents and roots of numbers can be produced by multiplying and dividing logarithms. I knew that if there was some easy way of finding the logarithm of a number, I could then create a calculator that could multiply, divide, and so forth without going through the endless number of steps of the other methods then in use.

After some research, I came upon a method of generating logarithms that required only a small number of steps. It is called the factor-combining method for finding logarithms, and it is based on a formula which cleverly uses just a few constants (previously determined numbers that can be stored permanently in the calculator) to generate the log of any number.

After some work, I found a way to adapt the factor-combining method of generating logs to the requirements of digital electronics. I could generate logarithms and then perform calculations using logic circuits that required less than three hundred transistors. This is a small number of circuits when one considers that today, even the smallest silicon chips contain several thousand circuits. Today, however, individual circuits have a negligible cost, while in the early 1960s transistors were not that cheap, and not yet that small.

To my knowledge, Wang Laboratories was the only company that discovered how to use the factor-combining method to generate logarithms. Ed Lesnick, an engineer who came to Wang Laboratories in 1968, says that when he was at Monroe, their chief programmer was still trying to figure out how Wang calculators generated logarithms.

The calculator I devised required that the user have some familiarity with the use of logarithms and the concept of a program, but it was still vastly easier to use than a computer. It could generate a logarithm with the punch of one key, and it could do it in fifty milliseconds. Equally important, LOCI could fit on the corner of a desk.

There were other innovative aspects of LOCI. I designed it so that it could be programmed and fed data in a variety of different ways. It could be programmed by punching buttons on the console, or by means of an attachment that allowed the user to run programs stored on punched paper cards. It could be purchased with a teletype, which could be used as both a terminal and a printer. Finally it could be configured so that several keyboards in different locations could serve as terminals for one LOCI. This approach reflected my belief that the customer should be able to both expand and upgrade a product and not be stuck with obsolete or incompatible technology. This has the effect of cementing the relationship between our company and a customer as time goes by, so that the customer's investment in Wang products increases.

On October 29, 1964, I applied for a patent for the basic processing unit of this calculator (the patent was awarded in 1968), and I promptly set about gearing up for production and marketing. Once again, we used the various trade shows and conventions to get word around about our new desk-top calculator. Because I did not yet have a marketing staff of any size, we marketed LOCI through manufacturers' representatives—independent agents who handled a variety of products from different manufacturers. We discovered that the market was indeed ready for us. Lawrence Livermore Laboratories of the University of California at Berkeley and other nuclear laboratories bought LOCI, as did a number of other research centers.

Still, LOCI was a sensitive instrument, and it required a sophisticated user, a point that was underscored by an episode in France. One of our customers there was the French National Railroads, who used the calculator to solve complicated scheduling problems. One day, we got an urgent call from the agent, who said that LOCI was producing inaccurate answers. We sent Joe Nestor, a high school classmate of Marty Kirkpatrick's and our jack-of-all-trades, to France to solve the problem. Joe and another engineer spent days checking out the machine, but they could find nothing wrong.

Finally, on a hunch, Nestor went out to the offices at 4:00 A.M. What he discovered was that the LOCI was turned off, something we had recommended against when we sold the instrument. LOCI used core memory for storage, and core memory tended to deteriorate at both low temperatures and high temperatures. At 4:00 A.M., the temperature in that office was in the forties. Nestor, who had by now turned from engineer into detective, waited to see what would happen. At 7:00 A.M., a janitor came in, turned on the lights, turned on the heat, and turned on LOCI. Nestor asked him what he was doing, and the janitor remarked that the crazy engineers who worked there left the lights, heat, and equipment on, and that the railroad just didn't have the money to pay for that kind of waste!

In fiscal year 1965, we sold about twenty calculators at an average price of just over sixty-five hundred dollars, even though we did not market them until the second half of the year. By 1966, we were selling about ten LOCIs a month, and the calculators were on their way to becoming the company's major source of revenue.

I recruited (I prefer the word *recruit* to the word *hire*: one recruits a colleague, one hires an underling) several key people during this period, including Joe Nestor and John McKinnon, an acquaintance of Joe's. I was flexible about what a person did and how they did it. People could move from one position to another quite easily. I was interested in finding out what a person's strengths were, regardless of what job they had. Today, there is more than one vice-president who came to Wang initially as a secretary or an assistant.

John McKinnon proved particularly helpful at finding building sites. Given our growth rate, this talent turned out to be crucial. In 1964, we moved the company to a facility we built on eighty-five acres in Tewksbury, the site of a former poor farm. A number of people were horrified that I had bought so much land, and several suggested that I subdivide it and sell off the pieces. At that point, Wang Laboratories employed about thirty-five people. The growth surge that took us from Natick to Tewksbury was such that many observers, including my wife, felt that the company had already seen its major period of expansion. Over the years, Lorraine has consistently argued for slower growth (and claims that I consistently change the subject when the issue comes up), and she recalls that when we moved to Tewksbury, she thought the eighty-five acres would be sufficient for all future growth of the company. I told the town selectmen that someday we might grow to employ a hundred people. In fact, spurred by sales of desk-top calculators, we surpassed that number within two years of occupying the facility.

LOCI was our first desk-top calculator, but its preeminence in the product line was to be short-lived. This was not because LOCI sales tailed off, but rather because LOCI became a transitional product that pointed the company in the direction of a new opportunity that would almost immediately dwarf sales of LOCI. This was the desk-top calculator called the Model 300. With its introduction, the growth rate of Wang Laboratories simply exploded.

While I believe that a company should not grow faster than it can manage, by no means do I want to suggest that a company should ignore all opportunities for growth. A company that vigorously pursues the development of new products will actually discover opportunities as a matter of course. But simply finding these opportunities is not enough. The CEO's chore is to judge which opportunities merit a major commitment of resources, and then determine how that market might best be served. Quite often these decisions demand that a company change the way it has been doing business.

I developed LOCI with the expectation that there would be a particular market for the machine, but once the calculator was out in the world, it became apparent that there was a potentially huge market for other calculators that I had not considered: a market that consisted of businesspeople and others not trained in the sciences or the use of computers, a market that bore little resemblance to the markets we had previously dealt with.

By 1963, Wang Laboratories had grown to the point where it seemed advisable to bring in someone to work on accounting and finance matters on a full-time basis. Before this, Malcolm Viar had handled our books. A young man in Malcolm's office named Martin Miller had worked on our account for a couple of years. With Malcolm's blessing, he came to work for Wang Laboratories full time in 1963. Malcolm himself continued to advise me until he died in 1986.

When LOCI came out, Marty Miller used to play with the machine during his lunch hour. At that time, Marty was about the only person in the company other than the secretaries whose background was primarily business rather than technology. One day, he mentioned in passing that LOCI would make a tremendous business instrument if it were easier to use. His remark piqued my interest, and through conversations with Marty and others, I set about determining what I would have to do to LOCI to make it attractive to businesspeople.

Since LOCI multiplied by first generating logarithms of the numbers to be multiplied, then adding the logarithms, and then generating an antilogarithm to display the result, it had the effect of producing an answer like 3.999999999 when you multiplied 2 × 2. While this answer might only be off by a factor of one in one billion, ordinary people feel more comfortable if they see the answer 4 when they multiply 2 × 2. So, we added a rounding function to the calculator so that users would not be startled by unusual looking, albeit accurate, answers. Similarly the keyboard of LOCI had a lot of names that might sound ordinary to an engineer but would seem exotic to almost everyone else. When businesspeople multiply, they do not want to deal with work registers, logarithmic registers, and accumulators; they want to type in the figures and read the result on the display. For this reason, we took a great deal of time reprogramming the machine to make its keyboard virtually self-explanatory.

A hard look at LOCI also told us that a commercial calculator would have to be simpler to maintain. The electromechanical calculators offered back then broke down easily—for instance, they would lock if you attempted to divide a number by zero. If we could make breakdowns infrequent and service simple, we would have a very strong selling point for those customers who were frustrated with the temperamental nature of competing machines.

Of course, we also looked at the electronic competition. There was an advertisement for the Friden electronic calculator in the *Wall Street Journal*, and so Dr. G. Y. Chu (an engineer I had recruited), Marty Miller, and I arranged to take a look at it— ostensibly as potential customers. An obliging Friden salesman showed us the machine. Apart from the fact that it was not that easy to use, its most glaring fault was its size—it took up half a desk. This led to the idea of separating the keyboard from the electronics package. The keyboard could be a small unit that fit on a desk, while the electronics could sit on the floor, serving more than one keyboard.

This idea led to another. While several users could use LOCI from remote terminals, they had to use it one at a time. Marty pointed out that having a number of users attached to the same electronics package was only really useful if they could all use it at the same time. And so we developed what is called a multiplexer, a device that would control traffic from the various keyboards that could be attached to a machine. All of this thinking was dictated by our efforts to see the product from the customer's point of view.

We also set about determining whether we might reduce the cost of producing each calculator. Rather than having a separate circuit board for each number on the illuminated display, I figured out a way to have one circuit board drive each tube of the display in sequence. By eliminating the extra circuit boards, we saved hundreds of dollars per calculator in production costs. Similarly, when we looked at the keyboard, we found that we could replace the expensive keys we used on LOCI with keys that cost one tenth the amount if we took the trouble to adapt the cheaper key.

With these and other savings, and with the economies we anticipated realizing by mass manufacture of the calculators, we were able to devise a desk-top calculator that was far easier to use than LOCI, and which we could sell at one quarter the price of LOCI. We called the calculator the Model 300. This was the first product made by Wang Laboratories whose end user could be just about anybody.

When it came time to price the calculator, we had a meeting to discuss the issue. The Friden calculator cost $2,195, another competitor was priced at $1,795. Someone suggested we price ours at $1,400. While we could have done this with no economic hardship, I argued strongly that we not do so. We were unknown in the general marketplace at that point, and my fear was that people would dismiss a new, low-priced product as a toy, or as an inferior product. Once we had established our reputation, we could cut prices without being misunderstood, but not yet. Hence, our initial pricing was just about at the level of our competition, $1,695.

We managed to design, manufacture, and bring to market the calculator in a very short time. Ten months after we began selling LOCI, the Model 300 calculator was on the market. Even though we started to sell it during the last six months of fiscal year 1966, its sales of $578,000 exceeded LOCI sales for the entire year. But its real impact was not yet evident.

Buoyed by LOCI and the 300, sales for the company rose from about $2.5 million in fiscal year 1965 to $3.8 million in 1966. Then in 1967, as we continued to expand the calculator line, sales exploded to $6.9 million—a better than 80 percent increase over the previous year. To make this growth possible, we had to do an enormous amount of hiring. From thirty-five employees in 1964, we grew to more than four hundred in 1967.

Ordinarily this kind of growth would have some impact both on cash flow and on earnings. However, in our case we showed solid earnings—equivalent to roughly 15 percent of revenues throughout—and only in fiscal year 1967 did our growth begin to stretch the limits of our cash flow. There were a couple of reasons why this period of rapid growth was more manageable for us than it might have been for other companies.

Because the calculator filled the void between the slide rule and the minicomputer, we were able to price it so that it would be competitive, but so that it would still yield gross profit margins of 65–70 percent. What this meant was that sales of the calculator generated a lot of cash, enough to finance anything short of the astounding growth of the late 1960s.

Even with those margins, we still kept a very close eye on costs. My philosophy has always been to make the most efficient use of resources in designing instruments, and, in part, that means anticipating the costs of producing a new product. The long incubation period of Wang Laboratories had honed our skills in predicting the costs of developing a new product, so that as we added to our line of calculators, there were very few surprises.

We were also helped by the nature of our business. Building the calculators was more a matter of assembly than it was of manufacture. We designed the circuit boards and had them manufactured by subcontractors. They would be shipped to us in Tewksbury, where Wang employees would assemble and test the calculators. This meant that growth for us was not so much a problem of capital investment as it was of finding and training people who could do the assembly work. It was true that as calculator sales soared, we had to add to our plant facilities, but in Tewksbury we had the room to build as we needed. Our original facility, built in 1964, had twenty thousand square feet of space. In 1966, we added thirty thousand square feet, and in later years we were expanding existing space by 150 percent every two years.

As sales of the 300 calculator continued to grow, we began to bring out other versions of the calculator tailored to specific needs. Besides a business version, we designed calculators for statistical uses, and for scientists and engineers. We also began to develop more powerful calculators with enhanced storage and more sophisticated programming capabilities. We created application packages for particular markets—a program to compute mortgage payments, a program for discounting bonds. This last application, which we will be looking at later, had some impact on the company's fortunes when we decided to go public.

At first, we had the market to ourselves, and so we moved aggressively to exploit each opportunity that we uncovered. The marketing of the calculator at that time consisted essentially of design decisions. We created the machine to serve a particular type of user, and once we made the machine, it sold itself. But no market is static, and it would have been foolish to believe that we would continue to have the market to ourselves. If we wanted to stay ahead, it was up to us to anticipate how this market would evolve.

We also had to take a look at ourselves as a company to see how well we were structured to take advantage of the opportunities we were uncovering. Prior to the 300, we had been a scientific company. With the 300, we entered the open marketplace, and this required that we become a very different company. Employees had to acknowledge the increasing importance of marketing, sales, and service, and in general a shift that was making us a little less like an academic research laboratory and a little more like an entrepreneurial business. Not everyone was comfortable with this transformation.

This was not unexpected. As a company evolves, there are always going to be people who like it for what it was, who will decide that they do not want to change. These people will leave to find a company more like their old company before it adapted and changed. On the other hand, I also tried to make it easy for those uncomfortable with these transformations to find some useful niche that would allow them to remain at Wang Laboratories. Of course, some employees blossomed in the new, more entrepreneurial environment, and I gave them the opportunity to move ahead no matter what their entry position might have been.

In any event, I did my best to ease the strain of these transformations. People were encouraged to vent their opinions, and I would try to marshal a consensus on major decisions. It is not productive to manage by laying down absolute decisions, particularly if they involve dramatic changes in the direction and nature of the company. We had many meetings during which managers from the various divisions had a chance to express their opinions and shape a decision. The result was that once a decision was taken, I did not have to worry about people second-guessing, or worse, attempting to sabotage a particular plan of action.

One of the more painless decisions we made was to formally establish an international division. I had explored overseas markets before the calculator—in the course of selling instrument packages and various other projects—but until we began to produce the calculator, there was no real reason to establish an international division. Our first international offices were in the United Kingdom, Belgium, and Taiwan. This list was not as arbitrary as it might seem.

The United Kingdom was a natural market for a calculator developed in the United States. After all, we speak the same language. I also had extensive contacts there from my earlier consulting work. In addition, it was one of the two countries in Europe at that time from which an American company might expect to receive fair treatment at customs. The other was Belgium. We chose Belgium as our entree point to the Continent. Given the rules of the European Economic Community, once we had exported products to Belgium, we might then resell them throughout Europe, bypassing tariff barriers that might impinge upon direct imports from the United States.

We chose to set up in Taiwan for two reasons. Not only were they a market for our products but, equally important, we gained substantial savings by moving to Taiwan some of the labor-intensive aspects of our manufacturing operations. For instance, we used magnetic core memory for data storage in the 300 series calculators, and manufacture of the cores was a very labor-intensive activity. The work required people with a good deal of experience at fine, detail work. Taiwan has an abundance of people well suited to this type of job.

When I established the international division, I also established a goal for sales outside the United States. If you look at the world market, the United States accounts for about one third of world commerce, Europe another third, and the rest of the world the final third. Ideally sales that reflected this distribution would provide a company with the greatest stability. However, for a company based in the United States, it is only natural that the percentage of American sales should be higher: a reasonable breakdown, I felt, would be 50 percent of sales from the United States, 25 percent from Europe, and 25 percent from everywhere else. The proportions for Wang Laboratories today are about 60 percent, 20 percent, and 20 percent. While we have not yet reached the point I predicted, we are not too far off.

Slightly more painful than the establishment of an international division was our reevaluation of our sales network. Demand for the calculators exposed glaring weaknesses in our sales channels and showed me that a network suitable for a small maker of specialized digital equipment was not entirely appropriate for a rapidly growing maker of widely distributed products. The question of sales channels posed a true test of the company's adaptability.

Beginning with the Weditrol units, we had used manufacturers' representatives as a sales force. However, now that sales of the calculator were growing, we began to discover that manufacturers' reps had grave limitations when selling to broad markets. And so, in 1966, I decided that we had to put together a national sales organization. This, of course, caused some disagreements, which underscored the tensions produced by moving a company from a scientific market into a broader arena.

One day, we had a meeting to discuss sales of the calculator. At the meeting were Larry Gosnell, who had put together our network of manufacturers' reps, Frank Chen, who was marketing manager of the calculator division, Ned Chang, who was project manager of the LOCI division, Joe Nestor, and myself. Larry Gosnell and Frank Chen saw the 300 series calculators as an extension of the LOCI. They made the argument that, this being the case, manufacturers' reps would be the logical sales outlet for the calculator. Moreover, Larry Gosnell and Frank Chen had picked many of the agents we were using and, out of loyalty, were reluctant to abandon them.

Because their experience with Wang Laboratories had been with a company primarily oriented toward specialized rather than broadly distributed products, there was nothing unreasonable about their arguments. But if, instead of looking at where the company had been, you looked at where the calculator was taking it, an entirely different landscape became apparent. While in terms of technology, the 300 might be seen as an extension of the LOCI, in terms of markets, it was a different animal. Frank Chen eventually saw this logic and adapted. Larry Gosnell never fully accepted this perception of the company and shortly there-after decided to leave.

I assigned Joe Nestor the task of building a network of Wang salesmen, and he spent the better part of the next year living on airplanes as he went from city to city, finding and hiring people. By June 1967, we had eighty people selling our products in forty cities. John Cunningham, who later became president of the company, was among the people we recruited.

Wang salesmen had to give up some of the perquisites of larger corporations, but they were recompensed by sometimes doubling and tripling their earlier income. At first, a salesman started out with a desk in shared office space. If his sales rose past a certain threshold, he could choose and rent his own office. A salesman's perquisites were based upon performance.

I also took a look at sales commissions and came up with a new way of rewarding salesmen. Because an executive is in a company that is ten times larger than another company, he or she does not necessarily earn ten times as much as the executive in the smaller company. Similarly I did not see that commissions should rise in straight-line fashion, particularly since our product virtually sold itself at that time. So I drew up a commission curve that grew according to the square root of the increase in sales. This meant that if you sold ten times as much as another salesman, your compensation would be three times as much.

At first, none of the salesmen complained because there was no competition and the calculator required little effort to sell. Later, as competition appeared, the salesmen began to complain, and I modified the formula, instituting a base salary and fixed commissions. The square root formula had been appropriate during the period when we owned the calculator market, but I had no trouble abandoning it when circumstances changed. Decisive leadership does not mean inflexible leadership. Had I stuck with my original formula in the face of competition, we might have lost a number of good salesmen.

The way in which we developed and sold LOCI and the 300 reflected all of the lessons we had learned about business and technology during the previous fifteen years: The more diverse a company's product line is, the easier it is to uncover opportunities. The more adaptable a company is, the more easily it can make the adjustments required to exploit the opportunities it discovers.

Had we not adapted the company to the needs of the new markets, we very likely would not have been able to establish ourselves in the market before competition arose to meet our challenge. Had we treated the new calculators as just an extension of LOCI and marketed them as we ordinarily did other products, it is probable that Wang Laboratories today would still be a small maker of specialized digital equipment. But I recognized that although this new calculator sprang from LOCI, it was altogether different from LOCI.

LOCI and the 300 marked key turning points in the exploration of digital electronics that I had begun when I first started the company. From the beginning, I was motivated by the idea of using the power of digital electronics to make people's jobs easier—to find a need and fill it. At first, I concerned myself with the needs of scientists and engineers. With the 300 series, I took this mission into the ordinary workplace. As we expanded the applications of the 300 series, we were guided by the idea that people do not want technology; they want solutions to problems. While we had to adapt as our markets broadened, the adaptation was not blind: the shape of the company might change, but not its soul.

Our long apprenticeship was over, yet the demands of competing in the open marketplace required one more fundamental change: the transformation of Wang Laboratories from a private into a public company. Going public was a spectacular success for Wang Laboratories, but looking back, I can see that it was yet another event in which luck and coincidence conspired in a most happy way.

9
Going Public

Going public has long been a rite of passage for entrepreneurial high-tech companies. In recent years, more and more companies have been going through this corporate adolescence at ever younger ages. In the early 1980s, it was not uncommon for computer firms to go public long before they had earnings, and in some cases, even before they had sales or products.

The late 1960s was also an exciting time for high-tech companies. The period has been called the Go-Go Years, and it was marked by inflated valuations much like those that characterized the new issues market in the early 1980s. It was in this market that I decided to take Wang Laboratories public. We needed capital to retire short-term debt, and to finance our growth, and I recognized that the mood of the times presented a great opportunity for the company. I also recognized that this mood might pass.

Unlike a number of companies that went public on the promise of great things in the future, when Wang Laboratories went public, we had solid earnings, very rapid revenue growth, and sixteen years' history as a private company. Since some other companies were going public with scarcely more than a letterhead, we looked extremely good in this environment. Going public was therefore a very happy and exciting event for us. It also turned out to be a very lucky event. About a year and a half after we went public, the Go-Go Years came to a grinding halt, and the new issues market all but died. Eventually a recession brought shareholders face-to-face with the reality that prices on the stock exchange were far higher than anything that might be justified by the prospects for earnings of the companies being traded. Stock prices collapsed, and although there have been speculative binges since then, the Dow Jones Industrial Average in constant dollars has never been as high as it was back then. Had we not gone public when we did, the capital markets might well have been closed to us for the next eight years, and our finances extremely stretched.

My decision to go public was based on our extremely rapid growth. I was not trying to cash in on the overheated new issues market. I was not interested in increasing my own net worth. Unlike many other entrepreneurs who look at going public as payday, I have never sold any of my Wang stock. Frankly I would have been happy if Wang Laboratories had remained private. However, the investments necessary to meet the demand for the calculators forced us to the limit of our credit with the First National Bank of Boston.

In fiscal year 1967, we sold $4,259,000 worth of calculators. This was eight times the sales volume of calculators during the previous year. At this point, calculators comprised nearly 62 percent of our sales. In anticipation of this demand, we doubled our work force to four hundred people and expanded our facility in Tewksbury by about 150 percent. It is a fact of life of business that you have to spend money for staffing and building before you reap the rewards of increased sales, even if people are begging to buy your products. We kept going to the First National Bank of Boston for additional short-term loans. By early 1967, we had already borrowed over a million dollars at a time when the net worth of the company was only about a million dollars. Our contact at the bank was Ernest Stockwell (who subsequently became a board member of Wang Laboratories). Peter Brooke, who was (and is) on our board, had earlier left the bank and was now involved in venture capital with the investment banking firm of Tucker, Anthony & R. L. Day. At the First National Bank of Boston, Mr. Stockwell was getting a little nervous because of the size of our borrowings in relation to the net worth of the company. In early 1967, he suggested that we go public as a means of raising capital so that we might reduce our debt burden.

For me, the crucial issue in going public was entirely distinct from the relative merits of debt and capital. Of most concern to me was the issue of management and control. I had already diluted family control of the company by the earlier alliance with Warner & Swasey. While James Hodge of Warner & Swasey had been a very positive presence on our board, I did not want to lose control of my company to an outside board of directors.

One of the reasons I founded Wang Laboratories was that I like to take my own risks. So long as I am in control, I have a stake in whether I'm right or wrong. I have never advocated venture capital because I do not want to be hamstrung by outside investors. Even if the outside investors are absolutely compliant, the fiduciary responsibility implicit in dealing with other people's money makes the CEO of such a company more conservative. This does not mean that I do not want to listen to other opinions. Indeed, I place great importance on communication within and outside the company. Nor does it mean that I do not feel responsible for the well-being of those who are affected by the fortunes of the company. It simply means that as CEO of a company that I founded, I want to be the final authority on any matters that affect its destiny. Furthermore, so long as I have control, I can never be tempted to abandon the business.

Apart from these personal considerations, I feel that there are other, practical arguments for individual control, if not ownership, of a corporation. For one thing, a CEO who does not have

143

to answer to outside directors for quarterly performance can lead the company with his eye focused on its long-term interests. This is important today since it takes a strong leader to balance the market's obsession with quarterly performance against the long-term positioning of a company. The CEO with control can also be more decisive and move much more quickly to take strategically important action than can the CEO who is second-guessed by directors and investors. Later in my career, there were a number of instances in which I was able to make such crucial decisions quickly, precisely because I had *both* the responsibility *and* the power to do so.

There is, of course, a converse to these arguments: a CEO answerable to no one but himself can destroy a company with impunity. Still, that is the risk of any corporate endeavor, and it is also self-corrective. Diversity in a free market economy acts to limit the damage that can be done by the incompetent or irrational CEO with total authority. People can leave a company and find work elsewhere, and customers have the option of buying from an alternative supplier. There are, of course, stories of abuses inflicted by privately held companies on communities they monopolize. But Boston is an economically diverse community, and high technology is a highly competitive part of that community. In this environment, the power-mad CEO would only hurt himself.

Every company has a set of goals. When I founded Wang Laboratories, my goal was for the company to serve its community and its customers, both through technology and through the positive economic dividends of its growth. I feel now, as I did in 1967, that I can best ensure that the company continues to pursue those goals through control of its policies.

Today, there are innumerable stories about founders of high-tech firms who find themselves ousted by dissatisfied shareholders. The question of whether or not these founders should be removed for the good of the company is moot, but it is certain that once a founder loses control of his company, he can no longer direct the company toward whatever goal he set for it.

This philosophy also influences the way I view the larger question of family control. As the founder, I would like to maintain sufficient control so that my children might have the chance to demonstrate whether they can run the company without fearing to take a risk or two. But the question of how far one should go to maintain family control of a publicly held company is a delicate one. All other things being equal, my children should be more highly motivated than a professional manager because of their substantial stake in the ownership of the company. On the other hand, I do not want to make that decision for my children. Nor do I rule out the possibility that a professional manager might prove to be the best steward of the company's future.

Today, both my sons work for Wang, and I have given each a different opportunity to learn about the way the company runs. Fred, who is now executive vice-president, has worked in a number of different divisions and has had a chance to see how every facet of the company works. Courtney has taken a very different route. He has asked for permission to form and control a small semiautonomous division of the company called Wang Communications, Inc., where he has the opportunity to show his entrepreneurial skills. Because Fred is the oldest son, he has a six-year lead in any effort to prove himself, and I am pleased that Courtney recognizes this. Juliette is still in college, and she has not yet decided what to do after graduation.

Beyond this, I have tried to educate my children as to my style of management, which is to lead by example rather than to dictate, and to leave room for individual initiative rather than to spell out every step of how a job is to be accomplished.

I want my children to have the opportunity to demonstrate their skills at management. In fact, I consider it their obligation—rather than their privilege—to do so. While I hope they succeed ultimately, the continued ability of Wang Laboratories to grow and serve its community is more important to me than who controls it after I retire.

It was with these considerations in mind that I weighed the question of going public. While lack of voting control may not automatically hamstring a CEO, given the choice, I preferred not to have to put that proposition to the test.

At that time, White, Weld & Company (now a division of Merrill Lynch) was perhaps one of the best-known investment banking firms when it came to bringing high-technology companies public. Through a contact there, I got in touch with George Montgomery, a partner at White, Weld who had had a good deal of experience in this area. Mr. Montgomery told me that it would be possible to take Wang Laboratories public and raise the money to retire our short-term debt without diluting the stock to the point where my family would lose control of the company. As it turned out, the period during which we chose to go public was perhaps the only time we could have done so and achieved that dual goal. This was because the hot new issues market was receptive to computer stocks at relatively high prices. I was also helped by a happy coincidence.

Apart from the fact that we were a solid company with good earnings and rapid growth, we were also very well known on Wall Street. Moreover, it turned out that we were well thought of by a group of people who could positively affect the fortunes of our stock. We owed this boon to our aggressive effort to develop applications for the calculator.

We would write particular programs that could be encoded on punched paper cards so that the customer who wanted to run a program had only to insert the card and enter numbers where appropriate. One of the programs would compute the present value of bonds. At that time, bond traders used tables to determine the value of a bond at a given moment for a particular coupon. The tables were much like the tables that banks use to determine monthly payments on a mortgage. These tables had been produced in an era of low interest rates, and so they were useful only up to 6 or 7 percent. But in the late sixties, interest rates suddenly exploded to 8 and 9 percent, rates for which there were no published tables. However, using our program for the calculator, a bond trader could discount bonds for any time period with any interest rate.

The calculator thus became a very popular item on Wall Street. One of the customers who bought the calculator was a trader at Salomon Brothers. He discovered that the bond trading program produced a different value for one set of numbers than did the tables that the company had been using for thirty years. Salomon Brothers got in touch with us and asked us to check out the calculation. We did, and felt sure that our calculation was accurate. Salomon Brothers then contracted a mathematician to verify the results independently. The mathematician came up with our number, demonstrating that the tables that they had been using for thirty years were inaccurate. The word that our calculator was more accurate than a bond table became part of the legend of the product and further enhanced the credibility of our company among the very people who would one day be trading the stock.

At the beginning of 1967, the company had issued 7,900 Class A and 34,474 Class B (nonvoting) shares. To go public, we would have to have a lot more shares, all of which were voting. So we collapsed the A and B stock into one class of common stock and then, in May 1967, did a nineteen-to-one split in order to increase the number of shares to a point where they might be sensibly priced and traded. In July, we distributed 716,856 new shares to the shareholders. This brought the outstanding number of shares up to roughly 1.5 million.

Given the state of the market and the financial community's high regard for Wang Laboratories, it was clear that owners of stock prior to the company's going public were quite likely to reap a windfall when the company did go public. I felt that the board of directors and senior people who had played a major role in the growth of the company should benefit from this event, and so, before the first split, I gave stock options to a number of the senior engineers and managers. After some consideration, I also extended the option to many junior members of the company. It might have caused resentment had one group of employees participated in this bonanza while more junior but still longtime employees were left out. I also arranged for employees to have the right to buy a certain number of shares at the issuing price. We ended up granting employees options for 20,423 shares at a cost of $4.17 a share.

When going public, you have to register with the Securities and Exchange Commission and also file what are called Blue Sky filings with each state. If a state feels that the pricing of an issue is unreasonably high, they might not allow you to sell your stock there. With roughly 1.5 million shares outstanding, our earnings came to $.50 per share. In White, Weld's judgment, twenty-five times earnings was probably the maximum acceptable price, given the state of the market, so we ended up pricing the initial public offering (IPO) at $12.50 a share.

At this price, we could offer 200,000 shares to the public and raise $2.5 million, which would more than allow us to repay our short-term loans. Moreover, a 200,000-share offering would still leave my family with control of over 65 percent of the stock. Because of my long professional relationship with Peter Brooke, I arranged to have Tucker, Anthony comanage the offering with White, Weld. The preliminary subscription for the offering was so successful that the two firms pressed me to increase the number of shares to 240,000, and I agreed.

There was one more delay before we went public. Chuck Goodhue had filed an S–1 prospectus (a statement about the company's business and its risks, including a detailed description of the LOCI and some of the original calculators) with the SEC. We had a long wait while the SEC approved the registration statement. Losing patience, Chuck called the SEC to find out the reason for the delay. Apparently no one could figure out what the company did. Chuck flew to Washington and, together with a salesman and a calculator, marched over to the SEC and demonstrated the instrument for the man who was reviewing the prospectus. That cleared up his confusion, and the last impediment disappeared.

Word seemed to get around that we were about to go public, and in the weeks preceding the offering, my secretary, Sybil Ashe, was deluged with calls from people who wanted to get stock at the offering price. All she could do was suggest that the callers contact their stockbrokers. One caller threatened to have her fired if she did not get him stock at the offering price.

Marty Miller went for a haircut one day during this period. While he was waiting for his turn, the talk in the barbershop was exclusively concerned with how to get Wang stock. He did not dare to identify himself for fear of being besieged with requests.

On August 23, 1967, a number of us gathered in Chuck Goodhue's office to wait for the telegram from the SEC that would certify that we could now sell the stock. It was like waiting for a baby. Shortly after the telegram came, we got news of the first public trade of Wang stock. It was at $38 a share—more than three times the price of the IPO. The stock ended the day at $40.50. Even in an overheated market, its performance was well noted by the financial press.

The company which on August 22 had had a net worth of approximately a million dollars on August 23 had a market capitalization of about seventy million dollars. Even with the capital raised during the IPO, the net worth of the company was still only about two dollars per share, and so the market valued the company at about twenty times its net worth. In other words, the market felt the stock deserved a price-earnings multiple of 80 that first day, which, even in the Go-Go Years, was more than four times the price earnings ratio of the average technology stock.

Wang shareholders, including myself, watched our personal fortunes increase in lockstep with the stock. There was jubilation in the offices. I remember hearing my secretary, who had exercised an option to buy a hundred shares, shout, "I'm rich, I'm rich!" A number of the employees did make a good deal of money, even if they did not become rich. The options Marty Miller received enabled him to buy his first house. In the following days, the stock rose even higher.

Not long after the IPO, I received a letter from a major league pitcher named Moe Drabowsky. He had managed to get two hundred shares at the offering price in August. This was a year that the Red Sox made it to the World Series, and although Drabowsky played for Baltimore, he still had an allocation of World Series tickets. Since he had benefited by buying Wang stock at its offering price, he offered to sell me his World Series tickets at *their* offering price, which, of course, was far lower than the prices scalpers were demanding. This was the first and last time I attended a World Series. I am still waiting for another opportunity to see the World Series in Boston.

Even though I had no plans to sell any stock, it was still an intoxicating time. The shares the family held, whose value on August 22 had been about a dollar a share (based on the net worth of the company), suddenly had a paper value of around fifty million dollars.

But there were other, nonmaterial gains that came from the IPO. Since I had been warned that I might encounter discrimination because of my company's name, I was pleased by all this demand for the stock, which evidenced the respect the business community had come to feel for a company bearing a Chinese name. I continued to hear people argue that I should change the company name to avoid discrimination long after we went public.

Several years later, when we were taking in between fifty and a hundred million dollars in sales, the question was raised again. This time, I was told that the name Wang would prevent us from establishing ourselves in the word processing market. However, virtually every American name has foreign origins, and the fact that Du Pont has a French name or that Levi Strauss has a Jewish name has not impeded their growth; I don't see why the fact that Wang is a Chinese name should impede our growth.

I also took a good deal of satisfaction in the fact that even though Wang employees made great gains those first few days, few of them sold their stock. There was a feeling that the company would grow, and that the stock might become another Xerox. (Little did I know then that the market value of Wang stock would one day exceed the market value of Xerox.) I think it represents a very strong gesture of commitment when employees resist the opportunity to reap immediate rewards out of faith in a company's long-term prospects.

During that first year, the stock rose as high as $120 a share, and the temptation to begin to take profits on their $50,000 investment, made at $.15 a share, proved irresistible to Warner & Swasey. We arranged for a secondary offering in May 1968, to sell some of their shares. As trustee for the Wang Family Trust, Marty Kirkpatrick thought it prudent to sell a little of the trust's stock as well in the interest of diversification. Consequently Warner & Swasey and the Wang Family Trust sold a total of 130,000 shares at a price of $67 per share.

These were the only shares of Wang stock Marty ever sold from the Family Trust. While this was entirely the right thing to do under the circumstances, in retrospect, the trust would have done better had the stock not been sold. At the time this book goes to press, Wang stock is selling at $20 per share, which, adjusted for splits, is still about twelve times the $67 per share the stock brought in 1968. In the same period, the proceeds from the sale of stock has appreciated by a factor of about six.

In January 1970, we had one other offering, again prompted by Warner & Swasey's desire to sell stock. By this time, we had split the stock on a two-for-one basis. Wang Laboratories decided to take advantage of this offering to sell 120,000 shares. We planned to use the cash to retire more short-term debt and pay for some construction. This offering was priced at $43.25, the equivalent of $86.50 per share before the split.

This was the last sale of stock we were to have for seven years. Shortly after this, both the stock market and the economy turned bad, and the capital markets were effectively closed until 1976. We considered a stock sale in 1972 but withdrew it because the market was so bad that the price we would have received did not justify the offering.

This event made it clearer than ever that we had gone public at just the right time. There was a very short window between late 1967 and late 1969 when the company's growth and the state of the stock market made it opportune for us to go public. Had we waited, and had that window closed, we probably would have had to issue more shares at a lower price. This, in turn, would have dramatically increased the dilution of the company's stock.

We could have survived without going public, but it would have greatly slowed our rate of growth. Moreover, we would not have had the funds necessary to seize our dominant position in the calculator market before larger, more established companies could respond to our challenge.

It would be nice to say that I knew this was our one opportunity to go public in a way that suited my purposes, but that would not be true. We did not develop the bond trading application with an eye to motivating goodwill among a constituency for

Wang stock, and I did not know that the capital markets would sour to the degree that they did in the 1970s. Once again I was lucky.

Even so, I can say that the way Wang Laboratories did business certainly helped to make the good luck that befell it during and after the IPO. It may have been accidental that the right people came into contact with the bond trading program card, but it was no accident that we developed it. We were combing the market for needs we might adapt our unique calculators to fill. By using logarithms, we could make calculations to ten-digit accuracy—something only mainframes could do at that time. Our technological prowess and our determination to find and fill needs put us in a position where we could benefit from lucky accidents.

The demand for the calculator that forced the decision to go public was not an accident either. It was the product of a long process of maturation during which the company developed both its knowledge of what people want from technology and its understanding of how to bring people what they want from technology in the form of products.

Ironically, although it was the calculator that first made Wang Laboratories known to Wall Street and the general business community, we stayed in that business for only a few years. In fact, I made a deliberate decision to get out of it, even as the market continued to grow. Like its predecessors, LOCI and the Linasec, the 300 series calculators were transitional products. But because these calculators were such a major part of our business, and because we were now a public company, the decision to move away from these machines caused a heated debate within the company.

10
From
Calculators
to Computers

Even as Wang was becoming known as the calculator company, I began to wonder how much longer we should stay in this business. While the logarithm generator gave us a temporary advantage over the rest of the marketplace, new technologies loomed on the horizon. I could see the day when the desk-top calculator would become a commodity, a point when the advantage would go to the low-cost producer. This was not a race I particularly wanted to enter: the winner would be rewarded with profit margins so thin as hardly to justify the effort. And so, even as we expanded our line of low-cost calculators to meet demand, we began to look for opportunities in more sophisticated machines.

One such opportunity was the development of a general-purpose computer—a project I had not really considered since leaving the Computation Lab in 1951. I had ignored the idea earlier because of the huge development costs entailed, and because of my belief that people want solutions to specific problems rather than general-purpose machines. My new desire to develop a computer did not signal a change in philosophy so much as an acknowledgment of changes in technology that narrowed the gap between what I thought people wanted from computers and what they could deliver.

Computers had developed considerably since my years at the Computation Laboratory. The vast increase of internal memory storage capacity had permitted the development of what are called high-level programming languages.

In the beginning, if you wanted to get a computer to do something different, you changed its wiring. The advent of stored programs allowed you to change the operations of the computer by changing the instructions in a program. At first, these programs were written in machine language, which is really just a codification of words made up of ones and zeros—the only language a machine can understand. As memory increased, people began to devise languages such as FORTRAN, ALGOL, and COBOL, which had more in common with the notation of logic and statistics. These languages were the link between machine language and the user. The user would write a program in one of these languages which in turn would be translated into machine language statements tailored to the hardware of a particular computer.

What this meant was that computers were no longer the exclusive province of specialists with the patience to plow through endless combinations of ones and zeros. Scientists and professionals could learn how to use such languages as FORTRAN and COBOL. Then in 1965, John Kemeny (who for a while was president of Dartmouth) and a team of researchers invented a language called BASIC. BASIC took the concept of high-level languages one step further than FORTRAN or COBOL. It was a language so simple that in a matter of hours novices could learn how to tell a computer to perform simple chores.

Until the advent of BASIC, I had believed that most people would gladly trade the flexibility of a general-purpose computer for the ease of the prepackaged solutions our calculators delivered.

Our calculators could be programmed, but only within a narrow range. BASIC radically reduced the effort required to customize programs for a user's specific needs. I felt that the time had come for us to consider making such a general-purpose computer.

Thus, the process of adaptation continued, even after we had made the transition from a maker of specialized equipment to a company with products in the open marketplace. Adaptation during this period meant getting out of what had come to be our biggest product line. As is the case in any evolution, this process involved a number of false starts as we experimented with different—sometimes overlapping—approaches to developing a general-purpose computer. In all, it took us four attempts before we got it right.

Our first attempt to build a computer was not much of a success. In late 1967, Frank Trantanella suggested that, by using the central processing power of our more sophisticated calculators and a bulk storage device based on the magnetic cassettes we were using to store programs in our calculators, we might come up with a small computer. When I saw the machine—called the 4000—in the spring of 1968, it was clear that it could not compete with DEC's PDP–8 computer. Faced with the limitations of the 4000, I realized that I would have to look outside the company for the expertise needed to design the computer and other sophisticated systems I wanted to build. Frank Trantanella did not agree with my assessment that the 4000 was inadequate, and ultimately he left the company. Later, he founded his own company, Tranti Systems, a maker of point-of-sale terminals.

One skill we needed was programming expertise. We had people who were quite adept at working with hardware, and at devising application packages for the calculators, but we did not have the programming expertise that would, for instance, enable us to design links between our calculators and mainframe computers. Nor did we have the software expertise needed to write the operating system for a computer that we might design.

In April 1968, I told Peter Brooke that I was looking either to acquire or to enter into a joint venture with a software organization. I wanted the company to be in the Boston area. Brooke immediately suggested I look into Philip Hankins Incorporated, a highly regarded company based in Watertown that was the largest supplier of data processing services in Massachusetts. Apart from the highly regarded software expertise of its employees, the company's principal asset was a rented IBM 360/50 computer. Among the people who worked there was John Cullinane, who went on to found Cullinet, a major supplier of mainframe software. PHI was strongly recommended for the work it had done for IBM as well as such companies as Arthur D. Little, the Marine Midland Bank, and the MIT Instrumentation Laboratory.

The more we examined the prospect, the more the combination seemed to make strategic sense for both companies. Philip Hankins would benefit from our financial strength and growing sales network, and we would benefit from the immediate expansion of the services we could offer customers, as well as from their programming expertise. Finally we would have access to an IBM mainframe on which we might run simulations as we designed our own computer.

After some negotiations, Wang Laboratories acquired Philip Hankins Incorporated, on June 20, 1968, for roughly 102,000 shares of Wang stock. At that point, the stock was selling for about $73 per share, which meant that we paid about $7,450,000 for the company. The acquisition precipitated a good deal of grumbling among Wang shareholders because the price was more than seventy times the earnings of a company that had almost no tangible assets, and roughly twenty-five times the company's net worth (based on stockholders' equity).

Obviously I did not share the doubts being expressed about the purchase of PHI. In buying PHI for 102,000 shares of stock, we were giving them roughly 5 percent of our outstanding shares, a ratio that closely approximated the relative size and profitability of the two companies. This is not to say that I was entirely satisfied with every aspect of the deal.

The purchase made a number of the top people at PHI relatively rich, and within a year, a large number of these people—whose expertise was PHI's principal asset—had left the company. Some left because they did not fit into the new larger company, but it is safe to say that many who did leave found the decision easy to make because they now had a good deal of money. The defections were irritating at the time, and it taught me the lesson that if you enter into a relationship with a company whose principal asset is people, you should do so in a way that does not remove all incentives for those people to continue working.

Still, PHI was blessed with a strong group of analysts, programmers, and managers below the top level of the company, and we discovered that these people could fill the positions vacated by the departing senior people. It turned out that they had the expertise we needed, and for this reason alone, the acquisition of PHI turned out to be well worth its cost.

During the late summer of 1968, we launched two other efforts to develop a general-purpose computer. Both produced machines, but for different reasons, neither of these machines had much impact on the computer market. One, the 3300 BASIC, while better than the 4000, still had serious limitations. We started to develop the other machine—the 700—as a computer, but shortly into the development process we changed it into a programmable calculator in response to a competitive threat. However, with each effort, we were learning more about designing computers.

The history of the 700—the computer that became a calculator—illustrates how we again had to adapt to a changing marketplace. It also shows how shadowy the line between our more sophisticated calculators and general-purpose computers had become.

My original thought was that we would build a computer that had more in common with machines like the IBM 360—IBM's principal mainframe computer at the time—than it did with previous Wang calculators. I assigned Frank Trantanella (who had not yet left the company) and Prentice Robinson, another engineer, to work on the hardware side of the project, and some of the programmers from PHI to work on what is called the microcode for the machine.

Although internal data storage had increased dramatically over the years, it has always been the most expensive, and the most troublesome, aspect of design. In 1968, magnetic core memory was still the basic internal storage medium for computers, although its days were numbered as work proceeded on semiconductor-based random access memory (RAM). The constraints of memory storage meant that if you could devise a computer that required less internal memory to accomplish a given purpose, it would put you in a very competitive position.

In broad terms, this was the rationale behind the minicomputer—the PDP–8—which DEC introduced in competition with mainframes in the late 1960s. At first, DEC had the minicomputer market to itself with this machine, just as we had a free ride initially in the desk-top calculator market. Through the use of microprogramming, we saw an opportunity to design a machine that could compete effectively against both the DEC machines and the mainframes.

The word *microprogramming* refers to a program that is wired onto a circuit board (or a semiconductor chip) and which organizes the basic operations of the computer into more sophisticated functions. The microprogram is generally housed in the ROM—

the fixed read only memory that rules the operations of the computer's internal circuits. In essence, a microprogram stands between a software program and a machine. Unlike the basic hardware of a computer, some microprograms can be changed by merely changing a circuit board, but unlike software programs, they cannot be edited at will. Because of this, some microprograms are referred to as firmware—something between hardware and software. The virtue of microprogramming is that it reduces the need for expensive internal storage. Instead of compiling instructions written in a high-level language, the microprogram interprets commands directly. The trade-off is that a microprogrammed machine is less flexible than a machine that relies on compiled instructions.

We had used microprogramming extensively in calculators, but nothing as complicated as that involved in a machine as powerful as an IBM 360. In 1968, Harold Koplow joined us as a calculator development engineer. He had been trained as a physicist, but at the time he joined us, he was a pharmacist. He was very bright, and I thought that he had the makings of a programmer. He turned out to have a gift for writing microprograms. Programming at that time was an art; some people seemed to be able to sense how to use fewer lines of code to get the computer to perform a particular task, and to perform it rapidly. Apart from this, Koplow also had a strong intuitive sense of the trade-offs one had to consider when deciding whether to use software or hardware to accomplish a given purpose.

In the summer of 1968, we had a contest to see who could microprogram one of the instructions for the new, unnamed computer using the least amount of code. Koplow won, and he was put in charge of microcoding the new machine.

However, as work proceeded on the computer, Hewlett-Packard suddenly announced a new calculator, their HP 9100 series. While it was priced higher than our 370 and 380 series calculators—at about $5,000—it had a number of features that badly hurt sales of our more sophisticated calculators. It had a CRT display which, while nothing like today's CRT monitors, still allowed the user to see three lines of mathematical operations. It could be programmed both through its keyboard and through the use of programs stored on individual magnetic cards.

It was imperative that we respond to this competitive threat, and we did so by redirecting the team working on the IBM-like computer. Although its architecture was still based on the IBM 360, we changed its specifications so that it would become a computer dedicated to scientific calculations. We also directly addressed the capabilities of the Hewlett-Packard calculator. While theirs could handle 196 program steps, ours would be able to handle 960 program steps; while theirs had a maximum of 14 storage registers, ours would have a maximum of 120; while each of their magnetic cards could hold only 2 programs, our machine would be programmed by magnetic tape cassettes, which could hold many programs at once. Until that time, magnetic tape cassettes had been used only for music and voice recording, and never for digital programming.

The only problem was that their machine was out and selling, and ours was not even partially built. We took a gamble anyway and announced the machine in December 1968, promising to ship the machines in June 1969. At that time, all we had was a plan and a wooden model that showed what it would look like and where the keys were. Wang salesmen taking orders for the new machines were to give customers a package of our other calculators in the interim.

June 1969 came around, and the calculator was not ready to be shipped. The hardware was working, but the electronics had not yet been miniaturized to fit into the console. Still, we had to demonstrate the machine to keep increasingly restless customers satisfied. Harold Koplow took the prototype with its clutter of electronic parts out to a trade show in California. He bolted the console to the top of a bridge table and then ran wires from the console through a hole in the table to a second table underneath, where the electronics were located. Our relieved customers saw a working calculator that was very much more powerful than the Hewlett-Packard machine.

We succeeded in miniaturizing the 700 and then gave prototypes to salesmen to demonstrate—again in order to keep impatient customers on board while we solved one final problem before shipping the 700. We had resisted putting in a fan because of its noise. While we worked on that problem, the salesmen discovered a routine that enabled them to demonstrate the machine without the embarrassment of having customers see it overheat. They would demonstrate the machine, and when they noticed it beginning to overheat, they would say, "Now let's take a look at what's inside" and remove the cover. This allowed it to cool off, following which they could continue the demonstration. Eventually we accepted the notion that a little noise from a fan was better than an overheating problem, and we began shipping the calculators. The 700 series became a very successful product.

Once the 700 was out in the market, we noticed something that all the more convinced us that there was a market for inexpensive general-purpose computers: people were using the 700 to *write* programs, even though the machine was not really designed for general-purpose programming. This was brought to our attention by the great increase in the number of applications written for the machine. The reason people would put up with the inconvenience of programming on a calculator with a tube display was that the machine was so much cheaper than the general-purpose computers available at the time. There clearly was a tremendous pent-up demand for computers.

The 700 was our last successful product to use magnetic core memory, ending a relationship with this form of data storage that went back to my first days at the Computation Lab. Not long after this machine came out, Intel began marketing a semiconductor chip that could hold two thousand bits of memory. We were the first customer for these chips, which we used in a new line of business-oriented calculators called the 600 series.

Had we wanted to, we could have marketed the 700 as a computer. In fact we could have marketed some of our other calculators as computers as well. We didn't because it is a lot easier to sell a calculator—even an expensive one—than it is to sell a computer. For one thing, we could sell a calculator directly to the user, and we were good at that. In contrast, in the late 1960s and early 1970s, the decision to buy a computer would involve top management at most corporations, people who were just beginning to know the name Wang, but who knew the name IBM very well. There would be committees and meetings with the company's data processing people and a great deal of deliberation about the machine's compatibility with IBM and which languages it supported. The same was true when selling to the government: use the word *computer* during a sales call, and all of a sudden, you would be awash with questions about specifications, requirements, and red tape. The decision to purchase a calculator could be made at a much lower level and much more quickly.

We had one more false start before we finally built a successful minicomputer. This was a machine we started to develop at roughly the same time as the 700. We called it the 3300 BASIC. There was no question that this was going to be a true minicomputer. We envisioned it as having roughly the same capabilities as DEC's PDP–8. The difference was that the 3300 would be specialized for BASIC, the easy-to-use computer language developed at Dartmouth. While more successful than the 4000, the 3300 still had its problems.

The means chosen to load BASIC into the computer was paper tape. The problem was that paper tape loads at the rate of ten bytes per second (which is extremely slow), and BASIC is a long program. Getting the 3300 going involved feeding huge ribbons of paper tape into the machine at a very slow rate. It took roughly forty minutes to load the program, and if something went wrong, you had to start the whole process over again. Another problem was that it used a teletype rather than a CRT as a terminal for inputting instructions.

In large part because of these input problems, we never sold many of these computers, although to my surprise, we kept getting glowing letters about the machine from a few customers in Australia, who had figured out a way to use it efficiently.

As we struggled to develop computers, our calculator sales continued to grow, but disturbing signs made me wonder how long the calculator business would remain profitable. By 1970, our sales had grown to about twenty-seven million dollars and we employed fourteen hundred people. Our earnings remained strong at three million dollars, but the price of calculators was plummeting as competition increased from other companies.

Most of this price pressure fell on the simplest of the calculators. By 1971, the base price of our 300 series had dropped to six hundred dollars. I met with a number of our senior marketing people to discuss the situation. Given present trends, I could see the price of the basic calculator dropping to a hundred dollars in the not-too-distant future. Another ominous sign was the imminent appearance of semiconductor chips that contained all the circuits of a calculator—large scale integration. Securities analysts knew about LSI, and they were constantly asking us what we would do to respond to the competitive threat it posed. Although no one yet had managed to put a calculator on a semiconductor chip, it was clear that it was possible and that someday soon we would hear that it had been done. When that happened, the calculator business would belong to those who made large scale integrated circuits—and that would not be us, since at that point we had no semiconductor expertise within the company.

Both these circumstances argued for getting out of the calculator business. On the other hand, calculator sales comprised a whopping 70 percent of our revenue. In terms of its importance to the company, our dropping the calculator business would be like IBM's dropping its mainframe business.

Still, after a few weeks' consideration, I decided that we had to do it. And once I had decided to get out, I spent another week considering how to do it. I decided that we should disengage in stages. That meant that we would stop pushing the 300 series, as well as the 200 and even the 100 series which we had just introduced. We would continue to push the 700, the 600, and the 400 calculators, which, because of their sophistication, were somewhat insulated from the pressure to lower prices. We also redoubled our efforts to find new markets we might explore.

This decision was not the obvious one for many of my co-workers. John Cunningham, who later became president and was then in sales and marketing, argued against it, as did a number of other colleagues. Calculators had turned Wang from an obscure maker of specialized equipment into an internationally recognized company, and it was psychologically impossible for some managers to consider abandoning this market simply because of increased competition.

They posed all manner of arguments: about the strategic importance of calculators, about maintaining our market share, arguments that instead of getting out of the calculator business, we should be lining up suppliers so that we could get into large-scale-integration-based, low-cost calculators.

Nothing I heard addressed the main problem with the future of the business, which was that since we were not a semiconductor manufacturer, we would be faced with continued price declines without being able to control the cost of a critical element of the calculator. In fact, had we bought semiconductor circuits from an outside supplier and stayed in the low end of the calculator business, we quite likely would have met the same fate as one of our competitors. The competitor was Bowmar Instruments Corporation, a company that went into the calculator business just as we got out. During Christmas 1971, they introduced the Bowmar Brain, the first LSI-based pocket calculator. They initially sold it through Abercrombie & Fitch for $250. The calculator had an LED (light emitting diode) display, and it had four functions: add, subtract, multiply, and divide.

Not long after this event, Texas Instruments, Hewlett-Packard, and a host of other companies entered the pocket calculator market with their own products. My estimation that prices would drop to $100 for a basic calculator turned out to be much too conservative. Within a couple of years, basic pocket calculators cost under $20, and powerful programmable calculators cost under $100. Today, calculators with the capabilities of LOCI, which sold in 1965 for $6,700, are the size of credit cards, and they are so inexpensive that they are given away as premiums. Bowmar, which did not make its own semiconductor chips, found it could not compete with companies such as Texas Instruments, which did. Bowmar wound up bankrupt.

The decision to move out of the calculator business was one case where Wang Laboratories' good fortune was a product of decisiveness rather than luck. Although somewhat obscured by the continued popularity of the calculators, the information justifying that decision was there to be seen. Even so, the decision was a difficult one, and it was complicated by the separate question of what new products could sustain the growth of the company. Fortunately, at that time, we had two separate product lines pretty far along in development.

One of these product lines was the general-purpose computer. After our earlier false starts, we finally began to make progress on a machine that looked like it would be a success. By mid-1971, this machine, which we called the 2200, was almost ready for shipping. It represented the culmination of the lessons we had learned in our three earlier attempts to build a general-purpose computer.

When designing the 2200, we paid particular attention to the question of inputting data and instructions, which had been such a sore point with the 3300. Instead of a paper tape, we used magnetic tape cassettes for storing programs, and instead of a teletype, we used a CRT as a terminal. (Shortly after its introduction, we replaced the magnetic tape cassettes with floppy disks for inputting data and programs.) On the other hand, we used essentially the same BASIC interpreter that Dave Moros (an electrical engineer from PHI) had created for the 3300. Only in the case of the 2200, we put the ROM on a chip and housed both BASIC and its interpreter in ROM, thus solving the problems of memory storage and loading BASIC. Moreover, in doing this, we created an early base of applications of what is called EPROM, or erasable, programmable read only memory. With an EPROM, you can continually time or update the ROM of a computer without having to constantly buy new ROM chips. Instead, the user can reprogram the EPROM. (I remember that I suggested to Robert Noyce, the founder of Intel, that they develop bigger EPROM chips at ever lower cost to take advantage of its flexibility by broadening its application. They did, but not aggressively enough to keep Japanese competitors from gaining a big foothold. Intel made a lot of money on high-priced EPROMs but eventually lost a lot of market share to the Japanese.)

The cost savings of our approach enabled us to design and sell the computer at a price that would attract the frustrated programmers previously writing applications on the 700. Moreover, it was a computer that had the convenience of a calculator. When you turned it on, the screen flashed *Ready*—ROM had done the start-up chores most computers require of the operator. When you wanted to load a program, you pushed a button that said *Load*. It was a general-purpose computer that worked like a calculator. Again, our primary focus was on user-friendliness.

Because of this, and in part to avoid the pitfalls associated with the word *computer*, we initially referred to the 2200 as a computing calculator. However, it was a true minicomputer, useful for general business, as well as statistical and engineering applications. First shipped in late 1972, it continued to evolve, and we are still selling the computer today. It accounts for only a small percentage of our $2.6 billion sales, but we sell more 2200s now than in 1973.

Although it might seem that we wasted a considerable amount of money before we developed a computer that we could successfully market, the actual expenditure of funds was not that great. All told, the first three projects consumed perhaps between six and eight man-years of labor, or, in other words, about $250,000. None of the computer projects involved a large number of people because I preferred to assign development projects to small, highly motivated teams. One of them, the group that devised the 700, actually produced a highly successful product, although not the product originally intended.

Moreover, mistakes and false starts are part of the process of innovation. If a company is diverse and healthy, no single mistake like the 4000 or the 3300 will prove fatal. Mistakes are only harmful if you don't learn from them, or if too much depends on the outcome of a single project.

The other product line that helped to fill the void caused by our gradual move out of calculators involved equipment for word processing. As was the case with our attempts to develop mini-computers, our move into word processing was not without its false starts. The false starts, however, were well worth what came later. Word processing proved to be the market that fueled the company's greatest growth and took us into the Fortune 500.

11
A Beachhead
in the
Fortune 1000

If one event stands out from everything else in the 1970s, it was the introduction of our first screen-based word processing system. From the moment it was announced, everybody seemed to sense that it was revolutionary. Its success was such that the press that had formerly referred to Wang as "the calculator company" now began to refer to us as "the word processing company." The introduction of this word processing system, called the WPS, also marked the end of a rough transition that started at the beginning of the decade.

The five years between 1970 and 1975 were something of a roller coaster, not just for Wang Laboratories but for the economy and society in general. The period saw two recessions, the beginnings of post-Vietnam inflation, the oil embargo, and the first and largest of the OPEC oil price hikes.

While society at large was preoccupied with the self-examination that accompanied the Vietnam War and Watergate, events were occurring in computer technology that would set the stage for the explosion of what has been called the Micro Millenium. These technological events all had to do with increasing the friendliness and convenience of computers: the development of microprocessors, the development of programs that allowed ordinary people to manipulate text and data on TV screens, and the continued development of external memory storage. That these developments would capture the attention of the American public in the way they did came as something of a shock to what might be called the computer establishment. An article in the industry trade journal *Datamation* in 1969 contained predictions for the next decade by various luminaries in the computer industry. Not one of the people polled predicted the vast impact that computers would have on businesspeople and office workers.

As the CEO of the company that perhaps best represented— and most benefited from—the revolution which brought computers to business, I cannot say that I predicted the extent of this change either. However, I knew that there was tremendous potential for the use of computer technology in the office, and Wang Laboratories was poised to exploit that revolution as it came.

This period also brought us into direct competition with IBM for the first time. In 1971, when we first entered the fray against IBM, the media regarded my decision to compete against them as a very brash act. At that point they were 225 times our size and controlled 80 percent of the market I chose to attack. Seven years later, we were the dominant company in this market, and in 1978, IBM was 71 times our size—still vastly larger, to be sure, but the gap was closing dramatically. The reason this competition with IBM was not the disaster many people expected was that I framed the competition in such a way that our greatest strength was pitted against their weakness.

In the late 1960s, I read a study noting that while the average factory worker is supported by about fifteen thousand dollars' worth of tools and machinery that improve his productivity, virtually the only equipment supporting an office worker is a four-hundred-dollar electric typewriter plus pencils and paper. Computers had indeed penetrated the business market—in the form of data processing and payroll applications—but they were not a presence in the lives of ordinary office workers. This said to me that the office was untracked territory when it came to the question of using technology to improve productivity. Moreover, there were more office workers than factory workers, and with every year, that gap would widen.

In 1968, I recruited three people to look for opportunities in data processing, telecommunications, and business. Ed Lesnick, the man in charge of product planning for business applications, spent some time looking at the types of things PHI, our data processing service organization, was doing. One thing that caught his interest was an on-line word processing program they had on their typewriter terminals. Provided by a company named VIP Business Products, this word processor was nothing like a modern CRT-based word processor, but it had a search function that could skip to a particular line number and a replace function, and it could justify text.

At that time, the word processing market was almost exclusively controlled by IBM, and most of the machines available simply automated repetitive typing chores. Without a CRT, editing was difficult. It seemed to me that word processing presented an opportunity, but in 1968, we did not yet have the technology to devise a competitive product, and so I temporarily shelved the idea.

Two years later, we did have the required technology, and I decided that we should go after the word processing market in earnest. What we had in 1970 that we did not have in 1968 was the 700 series calculator. During those two years, we had leased IBM's word processing system, called the MTST (Magnetic Tape Selectric Typewriter), in order to study its features and applications. Looking at that machine, we realized that we already had most of the components that would allow us to devise a better machine. The 700 calculator was designed to work with a Selectric typewriter (the same device used by IBM's word processing system), and it could receive information from tape cassettes. Adapting the electronics of the 700 to word processing was really a matter of rewriting the firmware housed in the machine's ROM.

In November 1971, we announced the 1200, our entry into the word processing market. The 1200 was really an automatic typewriter with limited editing functions. A secretary could type a letter on the terminal which would be recorded on a tape cassette. She (in the early 1970s, most secretaries were women) could edit the letter by using command codes, and when it came time to print copies, she could print error-free copies automatically at 175 words per minute. A search function allowed her to find and alter single lines of text, which in turn meant that she could store all sorts of generic letters and boilerplate text on tape cassettes that could be altered and printed as they were needed.

The system was extremely primitive by today's standards, but its superiority to an electric typewriter gives one an idea of the potential for productivity gains in this market. Our studies showed that the average 250-word business letter cost $3.31 to produce at the beginning of the 1970s. The average typist worked at the rate of eighteen words per minute for draft copy, and slower than that for finished copy. For all the difficulty of working without a CRT, and for all the expense of the 1200 as compared with an electric typewriter, the 1200 could still cut the average cost of a business letter in half.

Because this was the first time we competed against IBM, the press interest in our announcement of the 1200 focused on the bravado of a small company daring to compete with IBM. In fact, IBM asked to attend our press conference in New York, and when someone asked me, "How do you think IBM will respond to your product?" I replied, "There are two IBM vice-presidents in the back of the room. Why don't you ask them?" The two VPs turned a little green as the gathered reporters looked around to see who I was talking about.

My feeling was that IBM would not respond immediately. For one thing, although they controlled 80 percent of the market, the market was still a tiny part of IBM's world. We were tackling their little finger, not their right arm. Then there were my memories of dealing with IBM in the 1950s. Although they are formidable and aggressive, they are highly bureaucratic, and as a result they are sometimes slow to react. This last factor proved to be very important for Wang Laboratories as we entered word processing because our first product had some problems. It took us several years to develop our products to the point where we felt that we had something clearly superior to IBM or anybody else. During the years between 1972 and 1975, we were extremely vulnerable, and IBM might have ended our threat altogether. But by not developing their own word processing technology, they provided us with the time to learn from our mistakes and correct them.

Actually some of our problems with these early systems were caused by IBM. We used the IBM Selectric typewriter as a terminal for the 1200. We announced the machine in November 1971 and then spent the next six months gearing up for production. However, we were having severe problems getting the machines to perform well enough to pass our quality control tests. One problem turned out to be our fault. However, as we started selectively distributing the machines in the summer of 1972, other problems began to appear. During printing, the carriage of the Selectric tended to hop around. The cause of the problem defied our analysis, an analysis that was somewhat limited because IBM refused to supply us with specifications for the Selectric. The effects of these problems on revenues were a little more obvious.

While there was tremendous demand for the 1200, which we began to distribute on a rental basis, the hopping carriage produced great irritation among customers, many of whom responded by canceling the rental. In fact, at one point, we had an 80 percent cancellation rate. These problems were all the more serious because the 1200 was one of the key products we were counting on to carry us out of the calculator business.

Partly because of these problems and partly because of a generally soft economy in fiscal year 1972, we had our first earnings decline (16.6 percent) in the company's history. The problems continued. For a short time during that summer, we did not have one machine that could print with good quality. During the first quarter of 1973, we posted the first loss in the company's history. The loss was only $116,000, but I am quite sure that were it not for the problems with the 1200, it would never have occurred.

Finally Ed Lesnick called in a couple of IBM servicemen to look at the Selectric. They immediately noticed that a part called a carriage stabilizing spring was missing. They put one in, and the machine worked. They also told us that all the machines IBM produced for their own markets had this spring. A survey of other machines revealed that the spring was missing in every machine we had. There were other, less serious problems with the machines as well. Lesnick, who was by this time irate, managed to get through to the appropriate vice-president at IBM and said, "This is Lesnick at Wang. You people have been screwing us. You have been selling us a product knowingly with missing parts. We just had a loss for the first time in the company's history, and you're absolutely responsible."

The VP claimed that the Selectric we were buying was built exclusively for the OEM (original equipment manufacturer) market and did not require a spring. However, right after this, IBM sent a team of ten people up to Tewksbury to install the missing stabilizer spring in every machine.

Partly out of curiosity, and partly to determine whether there might be grounds for a suit against IBM, Ed tried to call Evelyn Berezin, the president of Redactron, one of our competitors. They also used the Selectric as the terminal for their automatic typewriting systems. Lesnick could not get through the secretary to talk to Ms. Berezin, and so he let the matter drop. However, years later, he ran into her and learned that Redactron had gone through the same torments with the Selectric that we had and had never solved the problem. IBM had neglected to tell them about the missing stabilizer spring.

While we were solving the production problems with the 1200, we were also considering the question of sales and marketing. We decided that the office market was sufficiently different from our previous sales arena to justify a separate sales force dedicated to selling word processing equipment. Also, because it was a product aimed at making a secretary's life easier, we recruited a good number of women to sell the machines. Many of these women had, in fact, been secretaries and understood the ways in which the 1200 might lighten the burdens of a secretary's job.

Despite our efforts to properly position and sell the product, the 1200 never really fulfilled the expectations I had for it. While it was an improvement over the electric typewriter, it still had some significant limitations. Without a CRT, it was difficult for the secretary to remember exactly where she was in the text and what she had done. Moreover, the editing commands required memory skills you would more likely find in a programmer than a secretary. Eventually we put a one-line CRT on the 1200, but this was still insufficient to facilitate the editing of whole documents as opposed to individual lines.

We put Carl Masi, who came to us in 1974 from Sanders Associates, in charge of our word processing marketing effort. Even with the limitations of the 1200, we were still well positioned in the word processing market by 1975. Then Xerox came out with their own automatic typewriting system—the 800. Although it was no easier to use than the 1200, it was based on a Diablo printer, which was twice as fast as our system. The speed advantage made it extremely difficult for our sales force to sell against the Xerox system, and they became increasingly restive.

To meet this threat and to address the shortcomings of the 1200, we began to think about developing a new generation of word processors. Only this time, we went about it entirely differently than we had with the 1200. With the 1200, we had taken advantage of electronics we had developed for other systems to devise a machine not dissimilar to automatic typewriters available at that time. It was not a machine that paid any great attention to the desires and limitations of the user. With the successor machine, we took an entirely opposite approach: a team under Harold Koplow concerned themselves exclusively with what a secretary would want from the machine, and only then did they begin to draw up specifications.

At that time, there were one or two CRT-based word processors available. They were made by such companies as AES and Vydec. Koplow and his team took a look at these machines but did not see anything worthy of emulation. Instead, they started writing a manual for a word processor from scratch. While they did so, they kept in constant communication with the word processing center at Wang. They continued until they had written a manual for a machine that any secretary could learn to use in about half an hour, but which still had all the features they most wanted in a word processor.

The new machine would be CRT-based rather than typewriter-based. This meant that the user could manipulate text by moving words as they appeared on the screen. A typewriter-based system limited the user to editing on a line-by-line basis, but with a large CRT, the secretary could easily work on entire documents. The most striking difference between this new system and the other CRT-based word processing systems already on the market was that it would be driven by a series of menus designed to guide the user through its operations. At every decision point, the secretary would be presented with a clear set of choices, written in a language anyone could understand. Getting the word processor to do what she wanted would be a simple matter of responding to these choices. The machine we envisioned would without doubt be the most user-friendly machine on the market at that time. It was perhaps the first computer with which an ordinary person could interact.

Only at the point when everyone who looked at the manual said, "That's a great machine!" did we begin to draw up specifications for the word processor. At one point, a marketing manager complained that the new machine would kill sales of the 1200. "Good!" I said, "Let's build it."

In the midst of this development in 1975, the company was hit by another financial shock. This time, the problems were directly attributable to the oil crisis of 1974. With the 1200 not living up to expectations, we were heavily dependent on sales of the 700 calculator and 2200 computer to continue to drive the growth of the company. By 1975, both the 700 and the 2200 had enormous libraries of applications programs, many of them written by customers. Two engineers from Westinghouse found it so lucrative to write and sell applications for the 700 calculator they had purchased for Westinghouse that they left the company and founded their own software house.

One application was the brainchild of Ken Sullivan, a salesman in our Chicago office. In 1969, Sullivan worked under Bob Doretti, who was then Chicago district manager. During a regular sales call, Sullivan spoke with an auto dealer in Joliet, Illinois, and during the course of their conversation, the man mentioned the need for a system to help salesmen comply with the newly passed Truth in Lending Act, which required that lenders acquaint the consumer with the true financial consequences of their purchase. After hearing from a couple of other auto dealers as well, Sullivan asked for a week off to write a program for the 700 that would perform the computations required by the Truth in Lending Act.

Even though he was a salesman and not a programmer, he was given permission to take a shot at writing the application. The application was introduced in February 1970, at the annual convention of NAAD, the National Association of Auto Dealers. The response among the twenty-eight thousand auto dealers gathered there was overwhelming and included commitments from some of the largest auto dealers in the world.

The dealers began to realize that in addition to helping salesmen comply with the requirements of the Truth in Lending Act, the program could be used as a selling tool. Automobile dealers often sell cars by arranging financing for their customers, either through the manufacturers' credit arms or through financing companies. Usually this process takes a day or two. However, the moment of an automobile sale is fleeting—if you don't have the paperwork for the customer to sign when he wants to buy, quite frequently you will lose the sale.

Our applications systems allowed the dealer to compute monthly payments for an auto loan on the spot. If a customer said the payments were too high, the dealer could refigure the contract instantly without having to ask for a day or two to redo the numbers. Moreover, while refiguring the payment schedule, the dealer could often find a way to come up with a payment schedule that would allow the customer to buy options within his monthly payment budget. Since options carry higher profit margins than the car itself, the package turned out to be a very lucrative tool for the dealers. Its appeal was underscored by sales stories coming in from the field. Dodge Chu, who was in charge of sales of the calculator in Hawaii, ultimately sold one of the systems to every car dealer in the state.

Then the large insurance companies became interested because the program could be used to compute and sell credit life insurance on accident and health insurance. Globe Life Insurance of Chicago purchased a hundred systems, which at that time was the largest order in Wang history.

By 1973, before the auto market crashed, various forms of the auto dealer package accounted for 70 percent of our business. These applications turned out to be another key event in the transformation of Wang from a company whose customers were primarily scientific and technical into a company whose customers were primarily businesspeople.

While the auto package produced a great deal of revenue, it also left us vulnerable when the oil crisis stopped automobile sales in their tracks in 1975. In fiscal year 1975, sales of calculators and computers still accounted for about 83 percent of our revenues, and so the 20 percent-plus decline in sales of the 700 due to the gas crisis had a real impact on earnings. For the year, earnings were off 33 percent from FY 1974. However, even though the period from 1970 to 1975 was marked by wild swings in earnings, revenues grew throughout the period. In 1975, our sales totaled seventy-six million dollars—over ten times our size when we went public in 1967, and about three times our size in 1970.

The intermittent squeeze on earnings forced us to substantially increase our bank borrowings. The combination of a rocky stock market and the depressed value of Wang stock effectively closed the capital market to us as a source of funds, and we had to turn to the banks to finance our growth. Although Wang stock never traded below its issuing price, it came very close to doing so during these years.

The problems resulting from the oil crisis also forced us to pare our labor costs. We reduced the salaries of officers and salaried employees, and we had to lay off forty people. I hated to take this step because it was the first layoff in the company's history. Happily, by the end of the fiscal year, we were able to rehire most of them.

By fiscal year 1976, these problems were behind us, and we started a period of growth that was unusual in the annals of American business because of the size and age of Wang Laboratories at the point at which this tremendous spurt of growth began. In FY 1976, our growth was stimulated by sales of computer systems such as the 2200 and the recently introduced WCS (Wang Computer System). But from 1977 onward, that growth was fueled by our move into the office market, a move presaged by the applications written on the 2200 for the business environment.

Although the 2200 increasingly became a business, rather than scientific and technical, machine, it was still a machine used primarily by small businesses. There were exceptions to this, of course. Stan Rose and Dick Orlando, who were then selling the 2200, convinced United States Lines to buy seven of our machines to manage some of their international port operations. The deal was noteworthy because IBM had virtually sewn up the contract when we began selling. IBM was unused to making a competitive argument about its equipment—ordinarily their reputation was their selling argument. We learned that it was possible to sell computers against IBM if you could force them to *sell* their equipment.

Although the 2200 showed up in some large businesses, the machine that really made us a presence in the offices of the larger, Fortune 1000 companies was our CRT-based word processor, the WPS. For this reason, the WPS had great strategic importance for the company.

We introduced the machine in June 1976, at the Syntopican trade show in New York City. This was the premier word processing show in the world. We had to rush to get a prototype to the show, and we had only three people capable of demonstrating the machine. But then something happened that showed that we had a revolutionary piece of equipment on our hands.

We had a small booth on the main floor of the convention hall as well as a hospitality suite at the Hilton, where the show was held. Word spread like wildfire about the machine, and within moments of the first demonstration, people were lined up ten deep at the booth. The hospitality suite became so jammed that we had to issue invitations in order to control the crowds. Despite the fact that it was just a prototype, and not even fully working (the printers were not operational), people saw text editing done on a screen, and they thought it was magic.

The three demonstrators were absolutely exhausted by the end of the first day, so that night Carl Masi had them train the entire New York sales force to give demonstrations. That it was possible to do this proved that the system was incredibly easy to use.

The basic equipment was so far superior to anything then available that even with a list price of thirty thousand dollars (for the hard disk version), one customer unflinchingly ordered a million dollars' worth of equipment on the basis of an advance look at the system.

Despite this word-of-mouth promotion and excitement, we still had problems getting our marketing operation in gear. Although we had a separate sales force for word processing equipment, the WPS initially was marketed in hodgepodge fashion. There were three dedicated word processing sales forces in Washington, New York, and Chicago, but in the remaining twenty-five-odd districts, word processing was under a district manager who also supervised data processing. As a result, there was no one looking out for and helping the word processing salespeople in these districts.

It was clear both to me and to our enthusiastic customers that the product was truly superior to anything then available in the marketplace, and yet it was being neglected by our own sales force. I was afraid that unless I stepped in and took some action, the machines might not have a chance to get established before our competition responded.

To resolve this problem, I separated the sales of word processing from the rest of the sales department and appointed my son Fred to head up this effort. This would indicate how seriously I took the new product. It was also Fred's first opportunity to show his mettle at running an important operation within the company.

These moves had the effect of letting Wang managers know about the strategic importance of the product, and within a short time, word processing equipment spearheaded rapid penetration of the Fortune 1000 office market. One by-product of this expansion was that our word processing sales force, which had been looked down upon by the computer and calculator sales forces, suddenly leaped to the front in terms of sales and earnings. One year, four out of our five top salespeople were women, and all five of them were selling word processors. This was particularly satisfying to me because I had long chaffed at the prevalent feeling back then that women were not well suited to work in high technology.

When selling word processors, we took into account the way Fortune 1000 companies make purchasing decisions. Many large companies demanded hard quantitative data on productivity before they would commit to a new technology. Rosalie Papoutsy, who had been my secretary and now worked on marketing the WPS, spent a good deal of time gathering this data, which became the quantitative argument for buying WPS. With these studies, we could make a convincing case to institutions like the First National Bank of Chicago that WPS would pay for itself in a predetermined time period.

Over the years, my wife, Lorraine, has taken it upon herself to remind employees of the importance of women to the growth of the company. Every year, we have a meeting to honor Wang Achievers—employees who have made outstanding contributions to the company. At these meetings, Lorraine gives a speech which has become something of a legend in the company. In it, she talks specifically about the role of women in the company, and about their role in the dramatic turnaround of word processing sales.

With word processing, we had a foothold in the Fortune 1000 companies. To consolidate that foothold and to heighten the recognition we gained from it, we decided for the first time to launch a national television advertising campaign. The idea that a computer maker should advertise on television was a novel one at that time. IBM advertised on television, but none of the other computer companies did. Moreover, television advertising was expensive. Essentially we had to double our yearly advertising budget in order to mount a three-month television campaign that consisted of a few strategic showings of a single ad.

The arguments in favor of this move, however, were compelling. At that time, we were the thirty-second largest computer company in the country. Most people in business could probably remember the names of only the top two or three companies. Television seemed to offer the best opportunity to leapfrog the companies in between IBM and us in terms of consumer awareness. Such awareness was important because of what has been called the "security blanket syndrome"—the essence of which is summed up by the sentence "Nobody ever got fired for buying IBM." If we were going to win over the cautious managers who tended to make the safest decision, we had to demonstrate that the decision to buy Wang was prudent, and this in turn required that we establish Wang as a well-known name in the marketplace.

The campaign was devised by Hill, Holliday, Connors, Cosmopulos, a Boston advertising company. It centered on one ad that played on the David and Goliath motif, David being Wang and Goliath obviously being the world's largest computer company. The ad featured a brash young man who interrupts a board meeting which is on the point of deciding to go with Goliath, and asks the question, "Have you considered Wang?" Then, despite glares from the intimidating group of businessmen, he goes on to confidently tick off the arguments for using Wang, gradually winning over the boss in the process.

Luck played a role in the ad campaign as well. Jack Connors of Hill, Holliday wanted to run the ad during the Super Bowl in January 1978. Because time was so expensive, we had to settle for the pregame show. To our delight, we discovered that the network ran the ad as the last advertisement of the pregame show, or in other words, as the first ad during the Super Bowl.

The campaign had the effect of raising our name above the crowd of other names. At the beginning of the campaign, Wang name recognition was about 4.5 percent among businessmen polled. The campaign raised that recognition level to 16 percent.

Before the TV ad, our salespeople regularly found their pitch stopped by the remark, "Wang? Never heard of them." After the ad, almost as regularly they would hear, "Wang? Oh, I saw the TV ad. Let me put you through to our office manager." We had bought an entry pass.

At first the competition ridiculed this strategy, but as our sales soared, companies such as DEC, Data General, Prime, and eventually Apple turned to television for the purposes we had used it for, though not always as successfully.

By 1978, within two years of our introduction of the CRT-based word processing system, we were the largest worldwide supplier of such systems. With fifty thousand users, we were also the largest supplier of small business computers in North America. We were now in a position both to protect our place in the word processing market and to expand our presence in the office.

It is ironic that today we hear that Wang is a word processing company attempting to break into data processing. In 1976, I had to put Fred Wang in charge of word processing in order to stress its importance to our field forces, who were only interested in data processing in small businesses. Few current employees or industry analysts are aware of this, but those of us who remember this struggle in 1976 are amused when we hear this characterization of our business strategy.

We had entered the office because we could make the lowest paid, least powerful, and most numerous workers—the secretaries and office assistants—more productive. We were later able to expand our role there to include data processing and communications. By being slow to respond, IBM gave us the time to invade this marketplace, which they had virtually locked up at the beginning of the decade. But because of the awe IBM inspires, our growing presence in the office went largely unremarked by the press. This is another problem that every computer company has to deal with.

Throughout the period we were establishing Wang as the leader in word processing, we continually heard in the press about how IBM was going to respond and crush us. Then, in 1985, when almost everyone in the industry was experiencing trouble, the press began to write about how we had lost our leadership of this market. Thus, we were acknowledged to have surpassed IBM in word processing only after IBM was presumed to have regained its preeminance. I am sure that other IBM competitors will agree that it is somewhat frustrating to contend with the press's obsession with the supposed omnipotence of IBM.

This is not to say that IBM is not a formidable competitor in any marketplace. When we chose to compete with them in word processing, I knew that this market was somewhat peripheral for IBM. But I also felt that there was opportunities in the market that IBM had not explored. Having dealt with IBM in the 1950s, I knew that they were not ten feet tall.

12
Keeping
Control

In 1975, I was faced with what seemed to be a dilemma. I was confronted with a problem that every founder eventually has to come to grips with: who will control the company's fate? My response was to make what was possibly the most difficult decision in the history of the company. Not the least of this difficulty was the fact that I made my choice in the face of unanimous opposition both within and without the company. Like many decisions a top executive is forced to make, this one involved a number of unknowns. But in the end, after listening to arguments advanced by my longtime friends and advisors, I decided to go with my instincts.

The financial state of the company in 1975 was not very different from what it had been when we went public. We had a good deal of debt, and we needed a great deal more cash if we were going to properly exploit the potential of our new systems. The difference was that now we were a public company, so we had the option of selling more stock. However, we had not exercised that option for the previous several years. The stock markets were essentially closed to us during the early seventies because the prices we could have gotten for stock were so low.

Now another consideration caused me to pause before selling any more stock. This was the issue of control. Because of the dilutive effect of earlier offerings and stock options, by 1975, Wang family holdings amounted to a little more than 52 percent of the common stock. Any additional offerings would dilute our aggregate holdings to less than the 50 percent required to maintain voting control of the company. This, then, was my dilemma: if I wanted Wang Laboratories to grow, it seemed that I had to relinquish voting control of the company.

Actually, by merely slowing the rate of growth, we probably could have financed our expansion out of cash flow. (In our case, the threshold for financing growth through internal cash flow was a rate of growth of around 20 percent.) However, this would have undermined the technological edge that we hoped the new CRT-based word processors would give us. We had to be prepared to seize the opportunity the word processor presented, and this meant a major expansion of the company.

The importance of seizing an opportunity was brought home by the experience of one of our competitors, Redactron. Like us, Redactron had entered the word processing market with a Selectric-based system, and like us, they had tried to develop a CRT-based word processor. Unlike us, they were sold along the way to a large company, Burroughs. The acquisition was friendly. Redactron appeared to believe that the larger company would help to finance their growth in this new market. Instead, the result was that the various layers of the Burroughs bureaucracy so delayed the development of their CRT-based machine that it was obsolete by the time it was released. Redactron never did establish itself as a force in the CRT-based word processing market. The high-technology marketplace is not particularly forgiving of companies that cannot swiftly develop, produce, and market a product.

If we were going to seize the opportunity presented by the CRT-based word processor, we had to return to the capital markets, and thus I had no choice but to confront again the question of control that had first come up when we went public. Nothing that had happened since we had gone public had changed my mind about the importance of maintaining my voting control of the company. The rough transitional years of the early seventies would have been rougher still had I been fighting with disgruntled board members who had the power to overrule or oust me. Without voting control, I might have been overruled on the decision to move out of the calculator business. Overruling me might have seemed reasonable to a board given the importance of calculators to our bottom line, but in the long term, it would have been disastrous.

The transition from calculators to computers and word processing required that we not be panicked by several quarters with earnings declines, and one quarter with a loss. Nineteen seventy-two, 1973, and 1975 each were bad years in terms of earnings. Had I not had voting control of the company, would the shareholders have had the patience to see the company through this long period? (Indeed, one of the largest investors in our original offering dropped out when we experienced our slowdown in the early 1970s.) Without voting control, would I have had the power to enforce the strategic commitment to word processing that turned out to be so crucial to the company's fortunes?

Instead, throughout this rocky period, I was free both to make decisions and to make them stick. I could act decisively and swiftly, without having to go through time-consuming political maneuvers to gain support. While the board of directors certainly differed with me on some of those decisions—sometimes quite strongly—the three proxies that voted Wang family stock were decisive when it came to the crunch. Perhaps the issue on which the board disagreed with me most vehemently, and hence the issue for which voting control turned out to be most important, was my idea of how to raise money without losing voting control of the company. In this decision, I was a majority of one.

What I decided to do was explore the possibility of recapitalizing the company in such a way that we might continue to issue securities, but that these new securities would have limited voting rights. Once again, I consulted with George Montgomery, the investment banker who had helped with the initial public offering, and who was then still at White, Weld. In the late fall of 1975, we had a number of meetings to discuss this issue. A group consisting of John Cunningham (then a vice-president), Harry Chou (then treasurer), Ed Grayson, our corporate secretary at the time, and I would drive down to New York to meet with Montgomery and other Wall Street officials to discuss the possibilities.

The issue was complicated because both the New York Stock Exchange and the American Stock Exchange have an identical rule which states that they will not list the common stock of a company if that company also has a nonvoting common stock. The rule also states that they could *delist* the stock of a company that issues a new class of nonvoting common stock. There were companies with common shares divided into two classes with different voting rights traded on the New York Stock Exchange in 1975, most notably Ford Motor Company, but those shares were allowed under grandfather clauses because they had been traded before the exchange instituted that rule. These clauses would not apply to Wang shares which at that time were traded on the New York Stock Exchange.

The first idea was to try to issue a type of participating preferred security which would have limited voting rights. Preferred stock is similar in some respects to secured debt in that it is senior to common stock as a call on the assets of a company. Typically preferred stock does not have voting rights, and it seemed that this might be the answer to our problem. Unlike bonds, the dividends on preferred stock can be omitted (although in most cases they accumulate if skipped) without courting the danger of a forced bankruptcy. The sweetener added for the holders of participating preferred stock is that they get a guaranteed dividend, plus whatever dividends are determined for the common stock.

Everything is relative in finance, and the attractiveness of preferred stock as a means of raising money depends largely on its cost relative to other means of raising money. The dividend rate a preferred stock has to pay is determined to a degree by how the stock is rated by the big security rating services such as Moody's and Standard & Poor's. If a stock is rated investment grade, it can be more advantageously priced than if the security is rated speculative grade. Unlike common stock, the price of preferred stock does not vary with earnings; it has a fixed value. In December, we went down to New York to visit the rating agencies with a proposal to create this new security. It was not a good day, and even as we spoke with the agencies, we realized that they were not going to rate the preferred stock as investment grade. We abandoned the idea of issuing a preferred stock.

After looking at other options suggested by investment bankers at such well-known houses as Goldman, Sachs, I decided that the best course would be the simplest but most controversial one: to create a B class common stock that we would issue in all future offerings. The new stock would have a higher dividend than the common stock, but only one tenth the voting power, although it would still elect at least one quarter of the board of directors. My reasoning was that given a choice, most investors would prefer capital appreciation and dividends to voting rights.

This reasoning did not win enthusiasm among the officials of the New York Stock Exchange. We were advised that the consequences of issuing this new stock would be delisting. While I thought that they would eventually relent on this issue, back then, they decided to take a stand on principle. (As this book goes to press, the New York Stock Exchange is finally modifying its rules on voting rights, having earlier relented in a number of cases, including the issuance of General Motors Class E stock.) In 1975, Wang Laboratories was not a particularly big fish, and it cost the New York Stock Exchange very little to close the door to us.

I decided to contact the American Stock Exchange and see what their reaction to the new stock would be. While they had the same rule as the NYSE, worded in precisely the same language, they found that the Class B stock would satisfy their requirements. Their interpretation was that since the new stock would have a fractional vote and, as a class, elect 25 percent of the board, it qualified as a voting common stock, and they would list both the regular and the B stock.

This seemed like a perfectly acceptable arrangement to me, but it was unanimously opposed by both my senior managers and the board of directors. Many of these people felt that it would represent a loss of prestige to move from the New York Stock Exchange to the American Stock Exchange, and thus that institutions would cease to look at the stock as an investment opportunity. There was also the fear that investors, deprived of the right to determine the company's fate, would avoid the stock and that we would have sacrificed the prestige of the New York Stock Exchange while paying an onerous premium for whatever money we might raise in the capital markets. Chuck Goodhue remarked at one point that he felt that the move would cut the price of Wang stock in half. Finally, some of the longtime employees in the firm opposed the idea because they had built up considerable positions in Wang stock, and they felt that I was putting their investments at risk in the interests of maintaining control of the company.

I listened carefully to all these arguments. Many of them were advanced by my oldest and most trusted advisors, and I would never ignore their advice. Apart from the general fear of the unknown because no one had done anything like this before, the arguments all seemed to revolve around the potential reaction of investors, arguments which involved the question of what investors want when they buy a stock. After several weeks of agonizing over these questions, I decided that nothing I had heard altered my judgment about the relative priorities of investors when they consider purchasing a stock. In any event, the debate was academic because I had the votes to enforce my decision, and on April 9, 1976, we voted to create the Class B stock. Initially we issued the shares as a stock dividend in the form of one share of Class B stock for every four shares of common stock held by shareholders.

After we came to an agreement with the American Exchange, we called the New York Exchange and told them that we were going to delist the stock and move to the American Exchange. The man in the listing group at the New York Exchange listened politely, indicated that he thought we were making a mistake, and then thanked us for the call and hung up. About two minutes later, Ed Grayson's office received a call from the same man in the listing office. He said that he knew I felt very, very strongly about the issue of control, but that if I thought about it, I would realize that I was making a mistake, and he just wanted to let us know they would not hold it against us if we changed our mind. However, I was not about to reconsider.

On April 21, with some trepidation, we awaited the first trades of the Class B and Class A (the voting common) stocks to see how the market would react. The Class A voting stock traded at about $13.375 that day, basically unchanged from the day before. The Class B opened at about $12.50 and traded at around that price for the day. The predicted sell-off never occurred. In fact, because the Class B carries a higher dividend than the voting stock, in recent years, it has tended to trade at a slight premium to the Class A.

The only problem was that at first trading continued to be heavy in the Class A and light in the Class B—just the opposite of the result we wanted. After some weeks, we figured out that even though we had created the Class B to be the actively traded stock, it was listed in the guides and newspapers below the Class A. Thus, when a client said, "Buy me some Wang stock," the brokers tended to buy the A stock rather than the B. We fixed this by changing the name of the Class A stock to Class C stock, which had the effect of shifting its listing to a place below the Class B. From then on, trading in Class B stock picked up impressively.

Adjusted for the one previous split, the opening price of the stock was equivalent to about $26, far lower than the heady values of the late 1960s. But the next year, both classes of stock began a steady appreciation, accompanied during the next several years by twenty splits and a number of additional offerings. Someone who bought a hundred shares of Class B stock on April 21, 1976, for an investment of $1,250 saw those hundred shares become two thousand shares worth $40,000 as this book goes to press ten years later. Those who bought Wang Class B shares in 1976 have prospered more than the buyers of the voting shares of all but a few publicly traded companies.

In fact, none of the anticipated disadvantages of moving to the American Stock Exchange materialized. On the contrary, since at this exchange we are a relatively big fish, Wang stock is usually among the volume leaders. We actually get more attention than we would had we remained on the New York Exchange, and we are treated very well by our specialist at the American Exchange.

The decision to create this new class of stock again underscores the importance of exploring every possibility, regardless of conventional wisdom. I found no acceptable solution among the options we first considered, but instead of compromising, I continued to look until I uncovered the appropriate course of action. In recent years, a number of the people who were critical of my decision at the time I made it have come to regard it as a deft stroke. For one thing, had I not taken the action I did in 1976, the opportunity in all likelihood would have been forever lost. Had I not done so, fears of diluting voting control would have inhibited us from going to the capital markets to raise funds and probably prevented us from using some of the more innovative financing techniques we have turned to in recent years. For instance, we have on many occasions issued convertible debentures to raise funds, something we would not have done if those debentures converted into stock with full votes. And had we not done this, we probably would not have grown as fast as we did during the following years.

But perhaps more to the point, during the last few years, the markets have been seized with a takeover mania that has distracted managements of major corporations and forced those companies wanting to remain independent to saddle themselves with debt or otherwise weaken themselves. The companies that have fought those battles and won, such as Unocal, CBS, and Phillips Petroleum, could hardly be said to be in a stronger position as a result. For a period of months in 1985, TWA management was virtually paralyzed by Carl Icahn's protracted and successful battle to buy the airline. It was reported that TWA's management was so preoccupied with fighting off Icahn and Texas Air that no major decisions could be made. The argument of the raiders is that management brings hostile takeovers on itself through incompetence which drives earnings and share prices down. While this is true in some cases, in other cases, share prices become depressed and companies become takeover targets because of market forces which have nothing to do with the competence of their management. Markets do not always appropriately value a company or management—no market is perfectly efficient.

In any event, the price of a stock—regardless of whether management is insulated from a hostile takeover—has the healthy effect of policing those who run the company. If they don't perform, outsiders dump the stock, and the insiders who hold the majority of the stock suffer the consequences. In the case of Wang Laboratories, the insiders include many of the employees of the company besides myself and my family.

Apart from this constant underlying pressure on management to perform, there is also the fact that the company bears my name. I take its health and performance personally. For all these reasons, I have more of an interest in seeing the company prosper than any other shareholder.

The result is that Wang employees can watch the maraudings of corporate raiders and acquisition-hungry companies with some equanimity, burdened with only the normal worries that accompany working in an extremely competitive environment.

By the end of 1976, Wang Laboratories had the capital structure and the basic strategic direction that have carried the company to this day. This is not to say that there have not been a great number of further developments in marketing, corporate structure, and products: we now do more business in two weeks than we did in all of fiscal year 1976. However, our business today is to a large degree an extension of the foothold that word processing gained us in the offices of the Fortune 1000 companies. Moreover, since 1976, Wang has done business with the question of control settled.

The process that brought us to this point in 1976 was evolutionary, not incremental. Except for the fact that I operated within the world of digital electronics, none of the several stages of Wang Laboratories can be seen as the *direct* extension of the previous stage. Each product cycle gave us a glimpse of new markets and new terrain that were not visible from the perspective of the previous product cycle. At the edges of each of these markets, we could see possible successors to the present product mix. Wang also became a different type of company as a result of the demands of these product cycles. We would see that the successor product cycle demanded that we increase the strength of marketing or finance or R&D, and when we were prepared, we would enter this new market. The company had to adapt to survive in each new marketplace we entered.

At no point during this process was I looking far into the future. I was instead looking at what technology might deliver to people three to five years down the road, and what that would require the company to be like in order to continue to grow and prosper. I have never thought that I had the wisdom to look further than five years into the future of the computer industry. Long-term planning at a company should be shaped by corporate philosophy—in our case, a twofold commitment to increasing productivity and making people's jobs easier. In fact, I did make one long-term prediction in 1976: in response to repeated questions from financial analysts, I predicted that Wang would be a billion dollar company within ten years. Given that we were one tenth that size, this was a bold prediction. Thus, it is not surprising that I was wrong. We actually crossed that billion-dollar threshold in sales within six years.

IV
Balance

13
The Modern
Company

The shape of the Wang Laboratories today reflects the lessons learned during its previous three and a half decades of existence. During that period, both I and the company acquired knowledge of markets, manufacturing, distribution, service, and finance—knowledge that enabled us to compete as the company evolved. Eventually this evolution brought us to a head-on encounter with IBM. Two decades after I first fenced with the giant company over the sale of my patent on memory cores, I again found myself having to deal with the vast arsenal of weapons that IBM has at its disposal. Only now I had considerably more resources of my own to bring to this competition.

Once we began selling our products to the Fortune 1000 companies, it was inevitable that someday we would run up against IBM's greatest strength: their influence over executives responsible for MIS, or management information systems. These are the people responsible for making decisions about computers dealing with data processing of various sorts: payroll applications, accounts receivable applications, and other major information needs within a corporation. Traditionally these applications had been written for mainframe computers, and since the late 1950s, IBM has dwarfed all other mainframe computer makers. In contrast, our entrance into the Fortune 1000 had for the most part been facilitated by office managers who were impressed with our word processing equipment.

As we saw opportunities to develop and integrate systems dealing with office information, we had to deal more and more frequently with people senior to office managers, and more and more we had to sell to people who had never considered that there might be an alternative to IBM.

The evolution of the company thus brought us into the most competitive high-technology marketplace there is. In addition to IBM—AT&T, the "bunch" (the other mainframe manufacturers, which today consist of Burroughs, Sperry, NCR, Control Data, Honeywell), the major minicomputer makers, and more recently some of the more successful smaller computer makers have converged on the office market. The aspects of this market that attract such a crowd are its size and the stability it offers to those who can establish themselves. As we discovered during the early 1970s, a company largely dependent on selling to small businesses can be whipsawed by events in the economy. Large corporations, however, have the resources to continue to invest in equipment that serves their long-term interests even if there is a recession.

Despite the intense competition, we had a great deal of success expanding in this market after our initial penetration through word processing. Today, in terms of numbers of work stations, we are the largest computer presence in the office. Before we went into word processing, approximately 80 percent of our revenue came from small businesses. Today, about 30 percent of our revenues comes from small businesses, while 50 percent comes from Fortune 1000 corporations. Another 15 percent comes from our Federal Systems Division, which sells to a wide variety of government agencies ranging from the EPA to the State Department. The reasons for this success have to do with our entirely different approach to office computing needs.

Originally word processing was a great opportunity for us because the office was new territory in terms of using digital information processing to deliver productivity gains. Apart from helping secretaries, though, word processing gave business a glimpse of the potential for using computers to improve productivity in other areas, such as communications and file management. Executives could see that word processing was just the beginning of what digital equipment could do to improve office productivity.

Rather than having to purchase separate systems to assist in the processing and sending of information, the ideal would be to have *one* terminal which could handle all the needs of an office worker, whether it be voice communications, entering or retrieving data, or sending reports. For instance, if Harry wants to call George, he should be able to do that from his one terminal without reaching for a telephone, and if, while on the phone, he wants to be able to electronically send some documents to George, he should be able to do that, too, without having to turn to another terminal. This is one of the goals of what is called office automation, and during the last eight years, this is where we have focused our technological efforts.

We converged on this goal from two different directions. The first had to do with the expansion of our word processing systems. To meet the demand for word processing networks that were larger than our hard disk system, we created OIS, or Office Information System. OIS was a word processing system that could be expanded according to the needs of the user. Because each component of the system—the work stations, printers, etc.—had memory and a microprocessor, it was easy to add on new components. Moreover, we made it very easy for a customer to upgrade from a simple word processing system to OIS. Over time, we expanded OIS by adding limited programming and data processing capabilities to the system.

The second prong in our effort to develop office automation products had to do with the evolution of our computers. Throughout the early 1970s, our staple minicomputer had been the 2200 BASIC. While, over the years, the machine has earned an enduring and loyal constituency, it had some distinct limitations as a machine for large corporations. As a computer dedicated to BASIC, it did not have the flexibility that would allow programmers to write applications in other high-level computer languages such as COBOL or FORTRAN. Nor did it have the internal storage required to run very large programs.

And so we set about to design a computer that would be more suited to office use in a large corporation. This was the origin of our VS line of computers, which today range from small machines to the VS 300, which verges on mainframe performance. The letters *VS* stand for *virtual storage*. Virtual storage refers to a computer design that allows you to run programs of any size, even of a length that exceeds the internal memory of the machine. Since internal memory is still the most expensive part of a computer, one advantage of a virtual storage machine is that it can handle mainframe-sized programs at a fraction of the cost.

We introduced the VS in October 1977. Because the machine was intended for a different market than any previous computer, we aggressively recruited salesmen with strong backgrounds in data processing. We did not want the VS to be seen as an extension of the calculator market. We wanted people selling the machine who had experience dealing with MIS executives, and who knew their way around Fortune 1000 companies.

Still, sales for the VS were slow at first. To sell the VS as a computer, we had to wade through cumbersome corporate decision-making processes. Then, in response to customer requests, we started adding word processing to the VS. This changed the way the machine was perceived. Instead of selling a corporate committee a piece of technology, we could sell departmental managers specific solutions. Suddenly sales of the VS began to take off.

By adding word processing to the VS, we enabled customers to integrate data processing and word processing. A year or so later, we added telecommunications, which enabled us to network a company's VSs and their mainframe computers. This was exactly the direction in which we wanted to head, but getting there meant dealing with delicate internal and external problems.

Once we added word processing to the VS, we found ourselves with two sales forces selling networked word processing equipment. We had a word processing sales force selling OIS, and a data-processing-oriented sales force selling the VS systems. Because a VS-based word processing system had the added attraction of data processing capability, there was a question about whether it would kill OIS sales. To minimize the potential conflicts, we ensured that neither purchase decision would mean scrapping previously purchased Wang equipment. We built a bridge between OIS and the VS, as well as to other Wang systems, such as the 2200. As it turned out, sales of both product lines soared.

We also decided that all present and future VS systems would be compatible, so that someone who bought the smallest system would be able to add on to that system without losing their prior investment. The trade-off involved in compatibility is that it ties you to a particular technology. However, with the VS, we knew that we had a design approach and an architecture that would not need fundamental change for a long time.

Internal compatibility was both a choice and a necessity for us. In the mid-1970s, we were a relatively small company. We had one basic research and development group, who worked on all our products. In contrast, IBM has long had the luxury of being able to assign different divisions to work on different product lines. While this makes for a powerful product-development engine, it has the disadvantage of resulting in equipment that is in large measure not internally compatible. For instance, you cannot upgrade from the IBM System 3 to the IBM 4300. The IBM System 36, which came out in 1983, is totally different from the IBM System 38, which came out in 1984.

While for us compatibility was partly a result of our need to get maximal use out of our resources, it has also produced large dividends for us as a selling argument against IBM. Wang users can buy equipment knowing that new developments do not mean that their old equipment will become obsolete. They can use our integrated systems no matter what Wang equipment they have purchased in the past. In fact, more recently, we made the decision that customers should be able to use our integrated systems even if they are primarily invested in another company for data processing, namely IBM.

While our efforts to make all our equipment compatible solved many problems associated with having separate sales and marketing efforts for word processing and the VS lines, we still knew that eventually we would have to bring these sales forces together under one roof. Office automation emerged as the industry direction toward the end of the 1970s. DEC announced this as a strategic goal two years before we did, but they failed in their implementation. We were concerned that they would try again, and we also noted moves toward office automation by IBM, Xerox, and some other large computer firms.

In June 1979, we held a press conference at which John Cunningham and Carl Masi outlined our strategy for the 1980s. We called it IIS, or Integrated Information Systems, and it involved a process of dissolving the differences between the word processing and data processing product lines and sales forces in order to achieve the goal of office automation: enabling an employee to access all the technologies needed to do his or her job through one terminal.

When we announced IIS, we were already delivering systems with a good number of the components of an integrated information system. It was not a case of promising to do something in the future; it was a case of providing a framework that allowed the world to understand the future developments of what we were doing at that moment. Because we were successfully implementing this strategy, we were able to identify Wang Laboratories with this concept in the marketplace. IIS was also a concept that was so simple and so in accord with the solutions-oriented philosophy of the company that every Wang employee could understand what we were trying to achieve.

While IIS offered a solution to the delicate *internal* question of how to bring together the divisions selling data processing and word processing equipment, our strategic goals in office automation also raised the delicate *external* question of who we would be dealing with in a major corporation when we sold our equipment. Initially our approach to office information stirred up a hornet's nest of bickering in large corporations over who would control purchases of digital equipment.

Mainframe data processing in the 1970s was done primarily by what is called batch processing. Different divisions of a company would feed data into terminals which would then be processed at the central mainframe. During busy periods, bottlenecks would develop at the mainframe as it tried to deal with the masses of data pouring in. For the manager this might mean a week's delay before he or she saw the results of a particular computer run.

In contrast, our systems were built around the concept of distributed data processing—an idea we pioneered in the office marketplace. Essentially it means what the words say: that data processing functions are distributed throughout the company at the departmental, rather than the corporate, level. The idea is that data processing should be available where and when it is needed rather than housed in one corporate department. For instance, in distributed data processing, the legal, manufacturing, sales, and payroll departments each might have their own system, equipped with interactive terminals so that instead of keying data in and waiting a week for the results, management might have information when they need it.

While this approach made us extremely popular with the departmental people, the traditional MIS people did not like the idea of losing control over data processing within their corporation. There are, in fact, powerful arguments for MIS involvement in these decisions, since a corporation with six departments did not want to be buying six different machines, none of which could talk to the other. This is a fight that still goes on today, although typically the solution has been for the MIS people to allow departments to make their local computing decisions so long as departmental computers are able to communicate with the mainframes and other computers within a company.

We have scrupulously tried to avoid being caught in a custody battle between MIS and departmental decision makers. We have dealt with MIS officials since we sold our first large systems, and we always stress that we will be successful to the degree that we make MIS departments successful. In other words, we try to help MIS departments understand the needs of the office, and bring to MIS departments ideas that will help them leverage their existing investments in mainframe equipment.

There were perhaps a couple of occasions early on when MIS departments snubbed Wang in order to assert their territorial rights, but that has not been a problem in recent years. A more persistent challenge has been dealing with the longstanding relationship between MIS departments and IBM. Many MIS managers essentially grew up with IBM, and it takes strong arguments to allay their suspicion of other companies.

Competing in this environment is a matter of delivering more than IBM (and our other competitors) at a significantly lower price. To combat IBM's overwhelming advantage in size, we can show a willingness to bring to bear whatever resources we have to solve a particular problem. In a number of large contracts in recent years, this has been the deciding factor.

In the early 1980s, we were negotiating a very large order with a Big Eight accounting firm. They had decided they wanted Wang equipment, but they did not want to have to junk several hundred IBM personal computers that they had previously purchased. While we have long been able to communicate with larger IBM systems, at this point, we had not yet accommodated the PC. We felt, quite simply, that we had a better product. By the early 1980s, however, it was clear that the IBM PC had become the standard for the personal computer industry. My son Fred was in charge of R&D at the time, and he saw that the issue was larger than this one account. He committed R&D to developing a link between the IBM PCs and our own equipment. This desire to accommodate the customer was the decisive factor in securing what turned out to be a forty-million-dollar contract. Ironically, after we made the commitment, the accounting firm decided that they liked our PC better, and they gradually phased out the IBMs.

More recently, our willingness to commit R&D resources proved to be the decisive factor in another very large contract. This time, the customer was one of the world's largest banks. The bank was ready to spend sixty million dollars for office automation equipment, but the problem was that they had wired their new headquarters building with IBM data cable. If they were going to buy Wang equipment, they insisted that we find a way to connect to their existing cable. This came up during a meeting with bank officials in Lowell, Massachusetts. While we were negotiating, I asked Horace Tsiang (who is now in charge of R&D) to try to devise a connection that would allow Wang equipment to use this cable. Before our meeting was over, Horace's group had actually built a device that the bank people could take back with them and try out.

The story also shows teamwork at its best. Not only should the sales, service, and support people work as a team in the field—and be known to the customer as a team—but the team concept should also extend to the relationship between the field forces and home office so that sales and service, R&D, and administration all work as a team.

The competitive battle against IBM dominates the agenda of any major computer maker in both the micro, mini, and mainframe markets. It is a battle in which the customers have a financial interest as well, and it is a battle in which IBM finds itself freed of many constraints that inhibited the company in the past.

Throughout the 1970s, a Justice Department antitrust suit restrained IBM from aggressive moves such as predatory pricing and announcements of products they had no intention of releasing (the idea being to freeze in their tracks buyers who might be tempted by some newly released competitive product). But IBM has had several good years (marked in part by the dropping of the antitrust suit) under the Reagan administration, and they have shown their power as the dominant maker of computers in all but one major market—minicomputers. While consumers might rejoice at the pressures driving prices down in the micro market, they would do well to consider the consequences of the disappearance of competitors to IBM. IBM has effectively eliminated the other mainframe makers as competitors. The net result of this is that IBM can price its machines so that mainframes yield the largest profit margins of any systems in the computer industry. The rest of the so-called bunch has every reason to go along with IBM, since they lack the power to improve their market share through a price war with IBM.

Just as Detroit would rather sell large cars because they yield the largest margins, so IBM would rather sell mainframes, and this has implications for the middle of the market. Given the company's ever-increasing stranglehold on the personal computer market, it is only in mid-sized systems that IBM is not yet dominant. It is in mid-sized systems that IBM has its lowest margins. This in turn puts pressure on the margins of every other maker. If IBM ever quells competition in this market, they will have both the power to raise prices in all sectors and the power to drive their customers toward larger systems. That has not happened yet because the minicomputer market is still healthy. This is good for the customer and good for minicomputer makers.

There is an even more formidable competitor than IBM, which my company as well as every other high-technology company— including IBM—must contend with. This is Japan. I refer to the country, not any particular company, because Japan's economic power is the result of concerted government action rather than entrepreneurial energy. Having both observed and experienced Japan's economic aggressiveness, I am led to the conclusion that they learned little from their experiences in World War II, and instead of tempering their imperial ambitions, they are merely pursuing their goal in the economic arena rather than the military one.

Wang Laboratories today has the momentum of a three-billion-dollar enterprise that employs thirty thousand people. This is, of course, very different from the company's earlier incarnations, as is the competitive marketplace in which we now operate. There have been stresses associated with the great growth spurt of the past eight years, but certainly none as threatening as those I faced in the early days of the company. The reason the company has been able to withstand the stresses of its evolution into a major industrial enterprise is that the spirit, or culture, of the company has not changed.

T he culture of a company evolves during its early years. In our case, this was not a conscious process. At first, the culture consisted of my values since, as the founder of the company, I could directly interact with our few employees. But as Wang Laboratories grew, these values diffused throughout the company to form what has been called a corporate culture. This culture is defined by the spirit and management principles of the company, and it determines whether a company will succeed over the long term.

For instance, the motto "Find a need and fill it" has guided the company for almost all of its history. It is a principle that every employee can understand—you don't need to go to the CEO to have it explained. Contained within the idea is the notion of individual initiative: don't ask whether something can be done; find a way to do it.

It was relatively easy to encourage that kind of initiative when the company was small. In 1965, when we had less than fifty employees, Stan Zlatev, one of the engineers working on LOCI, told me that the work schedule would interfere with a summer rental he had locked himself into months earlier. I offered him the use of my vacation house if the problems with LOCI messed up his plans. The gesture was real but unnecessary: it turned out that Stan worked right through his vacation.

As a company grows the CEO can no longer make such gestures on a day-to-day basis but instead must foster the spirit of those personal contacts that first formed the company's culture. For instance, we have formalized a number of the procedures that were carried out informally years ago. We now have a hotline which enables anybody who thinks that he has a good idea to bypass his immediate superior and communicate it directly to me. This means that a novel idea will not be lost simply because a supervisor lets it sit in his or her In box. Both the person with the idea and the superior know that another set of eyes will be looking at any idea a Wang employee thinks is important enough to commit to paper. The hotline also fosters sensitivity in the way supervisors deal with subordinates.

Many of our product lines have evolved from customer needs and ideas conveyed to Wang sales and support people. To keep abreast of these needs, we have a program called Wang Listens. When major customers come to our headquarters, we assign someone whose basic job is to interview the customer about the degree to which Wang responds to their needs, and to elicit recommendations they might have for us on products and service.

Even if employees know the mission of the company, however, the stresses of growth will still distort individual messages. When the company was small, I could talk to employees to hear their concerns and tell them what my thinking was on a particular matter. Today, that is much more difficult.

If company management and information flow is set up as though it were a chain, the failure of one link could lead to a temporary collapse. Our management structure is more like a weave than a chain. We have skip-level communication, which puts managers in touch with other employees more than one level away from them. This acts to correct for the idiosyncrasies of anyone's relationship with his or her immediate superior. We also have a good deal of horizontal communication between managers at the same level in different divisions. The net effect is to knit an information and management structure that is not going to collapse if one strand is broken.

There are times, however, when such institutional measures are not enough to maintain a healthy flow of information throughout a company. So many things happen at once in a rapidly growing multibillion dollar corporation that important messages can be lost or buried despite the best intentions and procedures. At times like this, the CEO has to be prepared to take extraordinary action. This is exactly what happened at Wang Laboratories in 1985.

I do not normally like to travel. Since I founded Wang Laboratories, I have done remarkably little business traveling. Indeed, for a number of years, I did virtually none at all. Beginning in the fall of 1985, however, I committed myself to a great deal of flying in order to visit field offices and customers. I changed my habits in response to what had happened to the computer industry and to my company the previous year. The industry as a whole suffered a retrenchment in 1985, an event so serious that it affected companies that had proven almost impregnable to previous setbacks. Wang Laboratories was among this group of companies. In the fourth quarter of 1985, we suffered our first loss in ten years, and only the second losing quarter in the company's history.

In 1985, we increased our expenses by 22 percent, expecting that sales would grow from $2.2 billion to about $3 billion in FY 1985. Instead of increasing by one-third, sales grew only 8.6 percent, to $2.4 billion. Had we budgeted for this increase in sales, earnings would have held up well, but as it was, there was a squeeze on earnings. Our profits were dramatically reduced. This forced me to make a number of painful decisions, including the first layoffs in ten years. I took this step with extreme reluctance. I feel that it is important for morale that employees trust their future at a company, and I hated the idea of taking an action that might damage that trust.

While a good deal of the problem in 1985 could be traced to a general cutback in spending on computer equipment, I also felt that some of the problem originated within our company. Things had begun to happen the previous year that suggested we had become a little complacent. Internally, this problem could be seen when the company missed delivery dates on a couple of strategically important products. Outside, the problem surfaced in customer complaints about support.

A few years earlier, in 1982, I had stepped back somewhat from the day-to-day operations of the company in order to give my executive team room to maneuver. In 1983, I designated John Cunningham as president. John, a Wang employee since 1967, came to the job by virtue of the work he had done building the sales organization of the company. He had shown that he could really motivate a sales force, and he also served as a superb spokesman in dealing with the financial community. In late 1984, however, as the computer business began to soften and our problems began to deepen, I felt that it was necessary for me to move back into a more active role in running the company. In June 1985, John left to accept an offer to become president and CEO of a much smaller computer company. He left because he wanted to run his own company, and because the situation he was offered promised the opportunity to amass a considerable fortune should the company do well. Rather than appoint a new president, I reassumed the title of president as well as the remainder of John's responsibilities. I felt that it was important to formalize the larger role I had been taking in the day-to-day operations of the company. Our employees knew that I had resumed a larger role in operations, of course, but I thought that it was equally important that the outside world be made aware of this, particularly since the entire industry was going through a rough period.

I had come to the conclusion that the key to the problems besetting us was communication. In 1985, we knew what our problems were and how to address them, but somehow the messages were not getting through: the urgency felt at headquarters about certain projects and procedures was not being communicated effectively to the field. The systems we had devised to make sure messages got through without distortion did not seem to be working. It became clear to me that something more was needed.

In business, nothing communicates the importance of a message more effectively than having the founder and CEO of the company deliver it in person. By the same token, nothing relieves the frustration of a field person or customer who has been having trouble communicating with headquarters quite so effectively as giving that person the opportunity to tell the CEO what is on his mind.

One aspect of the Wang culture that has developed over the years is what might be called a sense of urgency. As the company has grown, the increasing numbers of layers of management have had the effect of smothering that sense to a degree. Traveling offered me a way to cut through those layers. I have been able to both talk and listen to our people and customers. For them, my presence is as important as the messages I deliver. What I get back from these trips is not so much new information as a sense of the priorities of the concerns of our field people and major customers—a sense of what is urgent to them. The very fact that I do not like to travel—a fact that is well known—only underscores the importance I have attached to these visits.

My decision to travel was, of course, not the only medicine I felt was necessary to address the problems of 1985. But in many ways, it was characteristic of my approach to management challenges. I was willing to adapt when change demanded that I adapt. Among the other things I did when I reassumed the title of president was to acquaint those managers who had not previously dealt with me with my own particular style as a manager. I did not want managers holding back information under the misapprehension that there were things I did not want to know. As a manager, I pay great attention to detail; I want to know the details, not just the headlines. I am more interested in what is not going well than in what is going well. The growth of the company has meant that I have to delegate more and more of my responsibilities to my executives. Even so, I still expect to be in communication with them. I do not expect them to disappear and report back a year later.

Because my time is limited, I ordinarily do not get involved in the daily management of a specific project unless I think that there is a serious problem. If there is a problem, I will attend meetings until I think that the situation is under control. I do not take over the running of the meeting, however. I listen, and if something develops that I think requires intervention at my level—an extraordinary allocation of resources, for instance—I will step in. I will also step in if I feel that people are missing an important point. Even when I do not say anything, my presence has the effect of conveying to those gathered that I think the situation requires urgent attention.

In the spring of 1985, I attended a number of meetings organized to coordinate the roll-out of a new office automation product. While I mostly listened, on occasion, I stepped in to resolve a problem of resources or manpower. After a few weeks, no one in the company doubted the strategic importance of this product.

The shocks of 1985 had the effect of eliminating any vestiges of complacency within the company, and we entered 1986 with a renewal of the spirit that has characterized the company for almost all of its history. In January 1986, this revived hunger paid off when Wang Laboratories won one of the largest contracts ever awarded for computer equipment. Competing head to head against IBM, we won a $480 million contract to install MIS systems at United States Air Force bases around the world. The contract is about eight times larger than any previous agreement. It is noteworthy that we were able to underbid IBM and still price the contract so that we could make a profit. Coming after a tough year, the award has had a very positive effect on morale.

A management structure or theory is an abstraction, while a company is made up of people. When morale is good, an employee will often perform beyond expectations; when morale is bad, even the most brilliant organization will not be productive. We are a high-technology company, and as such, we employ all different types of people—from engineers in research and development to sales reps and secretaries. The various groups have different work styles as well as different needs and so demand different styles of management to maintain their morale and performance.

For instance, the engineers and scientists who conceive and develop our products are to me the soul of the company, and it is often worth one's while to tolerate behavior from a creative engineer that would be intolerable in an ordinary management structure. Because my own background is in digital electronics, I have always had a good rapport with the engineers who have worked at Wang Laboratories—even the most outrageous prima donnas. We speak the same language. This means that while on occasion I have had to make sure that two warring engineers were not in the same room at the same time, both engineers knew that there was someone at the top of the company who understood and appreciated their contributions.

Inevitably there are times when someone in research and development does his assignment well, only to discover that the company has decided to go with a different project for one reason or another. In such cases, I have always tried to find a particularly choice assignment as the next project for the disappointed engineer. Since morale directly affects productivity, it is no more than common sense to try to minimize the effects of potentially demoralizing situations.

I am usually willing to risk failure in the pursuit of a solution to a problem. For that reason, I am very tolerant if employees make a mistake, or even repeat a mistake, if they are trying to work something out. I do begin to get concerned if they repeat the same mistake a third time because this indicates that they are not learning from their previous errors.

Morale in a corporation is determined to a large degree by the way in which employees view their future at the company. Employees at Wang look at the senior levels of management and see them staffed with longtime employees from different areas of the company. They do not see many people who have been brought in from outside the company, nor do they see fast-track MBAs being groomed for rapid advancement.

I believe in repaying loyalty with loyalty. It is the nature of business that over the years a CEO will be tempted by attractive but somewhat questionable deals, and at such times, it is vital to have someone trusted around to point out ethical or legal pitfalls. One of the reasons Wang Laboratories has survived and grown for thirty-five years without scandal or catastrophe is that I have received sound advice throughout the period from such people as Marty Kirkpatrick, Chuck Goodhue, Bill Pechilis, and a number of other longtime associates. Marty started out advising me as a patent attorney, but he has been helpful in a wide range of business and personal matters. Marty gave me sound advice when the numbers were small, and he still does today, when the numbers are large. If at any point he had felt that the growth of the company had carried him out of his depth, I am sure that he would have told me so.

When I started out in 1951, I cannot imagine that many people would have seen me as a good candidate to run a $2.5 billion business. Yet I managed to learn what I needed to know in order to do so. I have seen many of my early employees grow with the company as well. My feeling is that you don't need special training to learn how to run a business. What you do need is the ability to observe, to test your theories in practice, and to learn from your mistakes. People with all types of backgrounds have this ability. If you look at the leadership of the

Fortune 1000 companies, you find large numbers of people at the top without formal business training—machinists and chemical engineers as well as salesmen and former mailroom clerks.

On the other hand, all too often, the newly minted MBA comes into a company with no thought in mind but a timetable for becoming president. I have come across many MBAs who have no particular love for the business they are in, or even the particular company they are working for. The business is an agglomeration of assets to be managed or leveraged rather than an entity that prospers because of the way it serves its customers. We do, of course, recruit MBAs, but they must prove themselves as anyone would, and there is no fast track open to the business-school graduate. Also I have learned that there are fewer surprises when you promote someone you know. You already have a sense of their weaknesses and their strengths and an idea of how they will perform in the new position. It involves far less risk than bringing a new person in to a senior position.

Because we are growing, we do have to bring in new people all the time, and at all levels. However, when we bring in a relatively high-level person, we bring them in at a lower level than the position we intend for them to fill. People need time to adjust to a culture and a structure, and so we do not burden them immediately with huge expectations.

The growth of the company has tended to give new responsibilities to people, even when they stay at the same level. Somebody responsible for a department of three people in a few years might be responsible for three hundred. Sometimes growth or promotions take people out of their depth, or into an area that calls for different expertise than they might have. If they are good, I will make every effort to find a position that suits their abilities. Because of this, we do not lose too many people who feel that their ambitions have been unfairly stifled.

Finally morale is affected by material gestures indicating that a company is concerned with the welfare of its employees. If a company is going to ask its employees to be something more than wage slaves, it must give them appropriate material rewards. With this in mind, I devised a program for employees called the long-term option.

The idea came to me one day while I was driving home from work on Route 128. It was in 1976, a time of high inflation. I thought that one way to both provide an incentive for longtime employees and insulate employee retirement money from inflation would be to grant workers an option to buy a number of shares determined by a percentage of their salary divided by the share price during that period. An employee would have to remain at the company for more than five years to have the option vested, and it might only be exercised after the employee reached the age of sixty. Because share prices would to some degree float with inflation, the long-term option would ensure employees of substantial gains. To the degree the company outperformed the rest of the economy, those gains would increase. To date, 6.5 million shares of these long-term options have been vested, giving the participants $53 million in gains.

I used to get a lot of ideas like this while driving home from work. This is one reason that my associates finally prevailed on me to accept a chauffeur. They were afraid that I would get so caught up in thinking about a problem that I might not pay attention to an oncoming truck, and they felt that it would be better for both me and Wang Laboratories if I did not drive while thinking about work. In general, I do not have much interest in the ostentation that is commonly associated with being the CEO of a large corporation. At any one time, I only own two suits, which I replace when they wear out. I prefer to have lunch by myself, and I generally use the time to read and think.

When I am away from the office, I rarely call in. My feeling is that if something important comes up, people will try to reach me—all too often, they do. Even while in the office, I do not do much business by telephone. I would much rather meet with people in person.

Wherever I am, I keep up a heavy reading schedule. Apart from the major local and national newspapers, I read a great number of periodicals and books. I studied technology during the age of vacuum tubes, but, partly because of my reading, I can still compete in the age of semiconductors.

I intend to continue to keep abreast of changes in the world and in my industry. At the same time, I intend to continue to foster the spirit that has enlivened Wang Laboratories from its earliest days. When I negotiated the sale of the patent with IBM, they were ten thousand times our size. Today, they are twenty times our size. If we continue to heed the lessons that brought us to this point, that gap will continue to narrow.

14
Responsibility

I think that corporate behavior should be judged by the same standards as personal behavior. I also think that both individuals and corporations have the responsibility to make some positive contribution to the world.

As the founder and CEO of a major corporation, I have a responsibility to the customers, employees, vendors, shareholders, and communities that Wang deals with. As an individual, I have a direct responsibility to return to the institutions and communities that nurtured and educated me a portion of the benefits I have derived from them. For this reason, in both my corporate and individual activities, I have taken pains to pay the greatest attention to the concerns and needs of those closest to home, which in my case is Boston and its surrounding towns.

At their root, my feelings about corporate and individual responsibility originate in a strong sense of loyalty I have always felt toward the people, communities, and institutions in my life. These feelings were strengthened when I witnessed what happens when people in power have no sense of social responsibility. I am referring to the abuses in the interior of China during World War

II. In the absence of a strong central government, the local generals acted only to protect their power and enhance their fortunes, and the immediate result was anarchy and suffering among the peasants. The long-term result was a revolution and a Communist regime that brought its own form of oppression. The corrupt generals ultimately brought about their own downfall, but not before they had inflicted great damage and suffering.

The lesson in this is that it is not enough to rely on outside authority to enforce moral or legal behavior. The compass of values has to be within a person or a corporation. Often one hears the contrary; that a corporation should be an amoral instrument, a money machine that maximizes its profits within rules set by the community. This argument holds that corporations that get distracted from this goal by social and community responsibilities end up making less money, which decreases consumer spending and increases unemployment and hurts those same communities as a result. My own belief is that just the opposite is true.

For one thing, no community can police an institution as well as the institution itself, and if a company places profits above ethics, then that organization will violate community standards no matter how stringently laws and codes are written. And those violations will produce demoralization of the work force, ill will in the community, and perhaps lawsuits that will have a long-term negative impact on the bottom line anyway. On the other hand, the company that orients itself toward serving both its community and its customers will reap long-term rewards in the form of loyal customers, peaceful labor relations, and positive community relations.

There is, in fact, evidence in support of this. A study conducted by Johnson & Johnson showed that over a period of thirty years, a group of companies selected exclusively because of their reputation for social responsibility outperformed both the Dow Jones Industrial Average and the S&P stock averages by an extremely large margin.

A number of American companies have consciously chosen to hold themselves to a higher standard of social responsibility than the law requires. Johnson & Johnson, for instance, asks its employees to read, study, and sign a written code of ethics. The company hopes that by doing so, its employees will adopt those values for themselves. I do things differently, but I endorse the spirit behind Johnson & Johnson's policy. My approach is to try to convey by example the ethical standards I expect the company to adhere to.

The very nature of business makes it all the more important that a sense of social responsibility be deeply rooted in a corporation. Throughout this book, I have written about the relativity of events, and about the importance of adaptability in both individual and corporate behavior. Markets change, tastes change, so the companies and individuals that choose to compete in those markets must change. The abilities that help one to compete in these changing markets change as well. There are times that call for decisive action, and there are other times when it is wiser to be more moderate. This continual flux makes it all the more important that two things remain constant. The company should never lose sight of the reason it is in business, and the people who run the company should never compromise their values for the sake of expediency. Without these, both a company and the people who work for it are in danger of losing their identity given the continually changing landscape they must negotiate.

This is not a simple matter, as anyone who has been in business knows. As a company becomes larger, the pressures of maintaining growth can begin to obscure the original mission of the company. Not everybody plays fair in the marketplace, and there is the continual temptation to respond in kind to dirty tricks, or to play at the level of the competition. For instance, as a multinational, we have the option of competing in a number of Third World markets where corruption and bribery are considered business as usual. Many companies accept the situation, however reluctantly, and let their employees know that they will not disapprove of surreptitious bribes if they result in increased orders. That is not the approach I have taken. So far, we have not established a Wang office in the markets where this is the most prevalent.

Then there are situations where the moral issues do not involve corruption, but rather questions of injustice. About ten years ago, I became uncomfortable with our owning a subsidiary in South Africa. As someone from a race which has suffered its share of discrimination, I could hardly ignore the abuses of apartheid. On the other hand, I felt an obligation not to abandon our customers or the people who worked for us, and for whom Wang was their livelihood. So we took the step of selling the subsidiary to the man who was managing it for us. This reduced our direct presence, although we still sold equipment through this distributor. We maintained this relationship until last year. I had hoped that things in South Africa would change over this period. But they didn't, and I began to feel that they never would unless people like myself made stronger statements. So I severed our last remaining connection to South Africa. Finally I decided that we had no choice but to do so.

Because the company bears my name, I cannot accept a lesser standard of behavior for the corporation than I demand of myself. My purpose in founding Wang Laboratories was to devise equipment and services that would increase worker productivity and make jobs easier. However, if in pursuit of this goal, my company exploited its own employees or its surrounding community, or pursued business in an unethical manner, this would negate whatever positive contributions the company made through its products. It has been said that ultimately all a person has is his reputation. In my case, that reputation is shaped not just by my actions as an individual but also by the reputation of Wang Laboratories.

Our reputation at home is more immediately determined by our relationship with our employees, our customers, and the other communities in the area. It is a relationship that is built on trust and understanding that derive from tangible actions we have taken to gain that trust. This is why I so resisted taking the step of laying off workers in the spring of 1985, a step that was forced upon us by the downturn in the computer industry. However, apart from this extraordinary event, our record is such that I am confident that understanding and trust will continue.

The layoffs also underscored the lesson that only by maintaining profitability can a company serve the people who depend on it. Within the company, I have tried to create programs that foster awareness of this fact on the part of our employees. Instead of a pension plan, Wang Laboratories has a profit sharing plan, a stock bonus program, and a stock purchase plan. The stock purchase plan permits an employee to option shares for purchase at 85 percent of the lowest price on the first or last day of every six-month period. We also have the long-term option which I discussed in the previous chapter.

These programs give every employee an incentive to increase the profitability of the company. In fact, most of the pressure for quarterly performance has traditionally come from inside the company rather than outside the company, since it is the company's growth that adds value to the stock and the options the employees hold. Longtime employees have had the satisfaction of watching their retirement money—their investment in Wang—grow much faster than any ordinary pension fund. Most employees realize that the continued growth of their investment depends on the company's continued growth and profitability.

People in the communities surrounding our plants and offices know that, having established ourselves in the towns around Boston, Wang has chosen to remain in that area. When we outgrew our space in Tewksbury, we looked for new places nearby where we could expand. In the course of looking for additional manufacturing space, we came across a handsome structure in Lowell. The building had been designed by the well-known Japanese architect, Minoru Yamasaki, and been built in the late 1950s by CBS Electronics, who had originally intended to manufacture semiconductors there. Since then it had been successively owned by Avco and Mostek, and in 1976, it was up for sale again. At first, our managers did not consider the building because it was so much nicer than the warehouse space they were looking for at that time, but one day, someone mentioned it to me, and I decided to take a look at it.

What I saw was a fine building and sixteen adjacent acres that promised room for expansion, all offered for a reasonable price. As I looked at the property, it dawned on me that I was looking at office space rather than manufacturing space, and that, indeed, from the workers' point of view, it made more sense to move the headquarters operation to Lowell and maintain the manufacturing operation in Tewksbury. Most of the manufacturing people in Tewksbury had settled within a few miles of the plant, while the senior management and headquarters staff lived much farther away. They were higher-paid employees, and they could better afford to live where they chose. While an additional seven-mile drive would not make much of a difference to them, it would impose a hardship on the manufacturing workers.

Lowell has a distinguished place in American industrial history since it was there that the Industrial Revolution came to America in the early nineteenth century. It was also one of the first planned cities in America, with an intricate system of canals and factories filling out the dream of James Russell Lowell. But at the time I looked at the property, it was a somewhat down-at-the-heels city that had been declining since its heyday as a textile center. It had often been cited as an example of the failure of the industrial cities of the Northeast to adapt to changes in the world economy. It was also a highly unionized city, with a government whose leaders squabbled among themselves while businesses and young people left in droves. Before we moved in, the unemployment rate was about 15 percent at a time when the rate in the state was 9 percent. Indeed, it hardly seemed an auspicious place to move one's headquarters.

But this is what we did, and we did not, as rumor has had it, do it because we were enticed by any special offers from Lowell. In fact, in 1976, when we purchased the property, Lowell was not particularly interested in us. They were looking to lure a larger, better-known company, and I think that at first they were disappointed that we were the company that purchased this choice piece of land. But our move to Lowell coincided with our most explosive period of growth, and so city officials were pleasantly surprised by our contribution to the local economy.

The original building we purchased had about 300,000 square feet of space, of which we occupied only half at first. Harry Chou, who was in charge of our financial matters, suggested that we rent the other half out, but I felt that we should wait before committing that space to someone else. Within a year, we had filled the remainder of the building, and we began to plan to build on the rest of our land. Because we needed a good deal of land for a parking lot, the only way I could envision meeting our needs for growth was to build upward. Unfortunately zoning restrictions limited the height of buildings to five stories. Thus, here was a case where we did need to ask a city for a special concession.

However, by the time we approached the city on this issue, we had already established a relationship of trust and understanding with both the townspeople and the city officials. As was the case in Tewksbury, we had taken pains to make ourselves a good neighbor, and in this case, the good relations paid off in the form of cooperation on the zoning issue, and city cooperation in arranging low-cost financing. The city must have been pleased that we planned to remain in Lowell even as we grew by leaps and bounds. For our part, we were confident enough that we would continue to have a good relationship with Lowell to commit ourselves to a major expansion there. Instead of moving our headquarters to a larger city, we set about building three twelve-story towers that dominate the flat landscape of the Merrimack Valley that surrounds Lowell. By 1985, we had expanded our original 300,000-square-foot presence in Lowell to buildings containing 2.3 million square feet of space, all within walking distance of each other.

Our effect on the local economy has been manifest. The Lowell unemployment rate is now about 3 percent, which is lower than the figures for Massachusetts and the nation. We are the largest employer in the community; moreover, a good percent of the decrease in unemployment came from businesses that sprang up to service the large influx of people and money that accompanied our expansion.

The positive effect of a manufacturing and development operation on an area stems from the fact that the money it and its employees spend, comes from sales outside the area. Unlike a retail operation, which takes local dollars in the form of sales and sends them elsewhere, to the manufacturers of the items sold, we are a source of wealth for the community. We are a net creator of jobs.

Quite often, Wang works on projects in concert with Lowell. A few years back, the city realized that it needed a major hotel near the downtown area if Lowell was to attract national and international corporations. Because the area was still run-down, however, there was difficulty finding the financing for the Hilton which the town wanted to bring in. I met with Senator Paul Tsongas (who was from Lowell) and Joe Tully, the city manager, and in less than ten minutes, we arrived at a solution. I decided to move our training center from leased space in Burlington, Massachusetts, to a new building we would build in downtown Lowell. Because people would be coming in from all over the country to use the training center, they would need a hotel to stay in while in Lowell. With this commitment, the group was able to obtain financing, and our building of the training center provided further impetus for the revitalization of the downtown area. Since customers and employees from all over the world come to Lowell for training, we spread the good name of Lowell far and wide.

As Wang Laboratories has prospered, I have prospered as well, and this in turn raised the issue of what I should do with my wealth. The needs of my children are adequately met by the Family Trust, and because we have no particular desire for a conspicuous life-style, the needs of my wife and myself are met by only a small proportion of our income. This means that I have the resources to begin to repay the institutions and communities that have helped me over the years through philanthropic donations of various sorts. I see this debt as real and material, and not something that can be dealt with by token gestures. In fact, for the past few years, I have given away more than I have earned.

I benefited greatly from my years at Harvard, but this does not mean that I was entitled to those benefits. Even had I not succeeded financially to the degree that I have, I would still owe a debt to Harvard. Similarly I have a less direct but nonetheless real debt to the Boston community as a whole.

In recent years, my major public activity has been in education. Today, our economy is even more knowledge-intensive than it was when I set out. Both personal and national success depend on a highly trained, highly educated workforce, and I have devoted a good deal of effort to try and help us achieve that goal.

My first public position in education was as a member of the Massachusetts Board of Higher Education. Later, I served on the Massachusetts Board of Regents, as a trustee of Northeastern University and Boston College, and as an overseer of Harvard University. As I became familiar with the problems of higher education, I began to wonder whether there was some need in this area that I could help to fill.

Boston and its environs contain perhaps the greatest concentration of educational institutions in the country, and the last thing I wanted to do was to set up an institution that would compete directly with one of the existing universities. The most likely prospect seemed to be in the area of graduate studies. I knew that a number of local institutions had dropped graduate programs of various sorts, and this being the case, no one could be upset should someone want to start a new graduate program.

I also wanted to make some contribution to the study of computer science. Computer science has become very popular on campuses during the past few years, but while universities have devoted enormous resources to the subject, there are still gaps. One has to do with optimizing the design and efficiency of software. Software is what makes computers useful and friendly, and so software engineering seemed to be a promising place to start. At Wang, as at any other major computer company, there are people who, although they lack training in computer science, find that they have a particular gift for programming. It is these people who would gain the most from taking time off to advance their knowledge of software engineering.

The idea of founding an institute coincidentally provided the answer to the vexing question of what would happen to the bulk of my Wang stock when I died. I wanted to give my stock away, but not in a way that would disrupt the markets. There was a strong possibility that a distressed sale of Wang stock would have a negative impact on the value of the stock and options held by the employees, who looked to the stock as their retirement money.

Thus the question of my estate involved my responsibility to all other owners of Wang stock.

The solution came to me while Lorraine and I were on a cruise to the Caribbean and South America in February 1979. During the cruise, I remembered that an educational institution could receive stock, even in a closely held corporation without having to dispose of it within a year as a foundation would. I thus had a solution that would allow me to contribute to education and solve the problem of my estate as well.

During my vacation, I came up with the basic outlines of the institute I wanted to start, and when I returned, I set about rapidly to get it going. By April 1979, I had organized the institute board, and by June 1979, we had state approval to grant a master's degree in software engineering. We found a campus in the form of a former Marist seminary in Tyngsboro, Massachusetts, which is near the New Hampshire border while also being convenient to Route 128 and Route 495, the main roads of Boston's high-technology industry. The former seminary is set on over two hundred parklike acres and seemed like the perfect spot for the Wang Institute. In January 1981, the Wang Institute began classes for its initial class of five students.

Over the years, the school has gradually grown, drawing full- and part-time students from DEC, Raytheon, Bell Labs, and Hewlett-Packard as well as from Wang. In the not too distant future, the institute will begin to offer courses in a much broader range of subjects. But even as it is now, it has justified my hopes for it by serving both the needs of the students and the needs of corporations whose employees benefit from its programs.

In a number of other projects, I have merged my interest in education with my wish to improve understanding between Chinese and Western societies. The Wang Institute has started a Chinese Fellowship Program which offers post-doctoral support to individuals in Chinese studies. A second phase of the program will be to offer similar support to scholars from seven institutions in Asia. At MIT, I have funded a program which offers fellowships to engineers from mainland China. In the cultural area, I stipulated that a million dollars of the money I have given to Harvard be used in support·of the Fairbank Center, which promotes Chinese studies, and in Boston, I am a major benefactor of the Chinese Cultural Institute, which seeks through exhibitions and other programs to foster a better understanding of Chinese culture. I am sure that in time I will discover other opportunities to contribute to education and cross-cultural understanding.

Apart from education, I have concentrated my philanthropy in two other areas, the arts and health care. In 1983, Jack Connors of Hill, Holliday was involved in an attempt to figure out what to do with Boston's Metropolitan Center, a breathtaking theater and concert hall that was suffering the effects of long-deferred maintenance. He asked whether I might help out, and I was instantly taken with the idea. As a company, Wang had long used the cultural and educational amenities of Boston as a recruiting argument when we were looking for people. Along with everyone else, we had taken advantage of such institutions as the Museum of Science, the Museum of Fine Arts, the Boston Symphony, and the Boston Ballet, all of which had been housed and were largely maintained by fortunes donated by earlier generations. These fortunes had been made in textiles, machine tools, and a number of other industries that, with few exceptions, were dying out in the area. As of 1983, there had been little philanthropic input from people in high-technology industries.

What we had was a situation where we in high technology benefited from the advantages of Boston without supporting the institutions, and I thought that this was wrong. I felt that by donating money to the Metropolitan Center, I might be able to induce some of the other newly wealthy people in my industry to follow suit. I talked the idea over with Lorraine, and together we agreed to endow the center. Lorraine put up one quarter of the money, and I put up the remaining three quarters. It took one day for us to commit ourselves to this project.

In all, we donated four million dollars to the center; however, we structured the donation so that the money would have the maximum leverage. We made the four million dollars a challenge grant, which meant that the amount had to be matched by other donations. When it received our grant, the center was deeply in debt to banks and other creditors, and so I also attached the condition that the banks make a concession of a two million dollar reduction in what they were owed. The four million dollars thus generated ten million dollars in benefits for the center. Today, the Wang Center attracts audiences for concerts of all kinds, ranging from classical music, to dance, to rock.

Lorraine and I discuss all of our philanthropic ventures. While I have led the way in some, she has proposed others. We both wanted to make some contribution to health care in the Boston area, but it took some time to find the proper charity. Rather than give money for research, we wanted to make sure our money would have immediate, practical benefits for the broadest number of people. Lorraine found the perfect vehicle for accomplishing this end in the form of the outpatient care unit of Massachusetts General Hospital. The outpatient care unit makes the medical expertise of Mass General available to more than 450,000 people each year.

The theme of my philanthropy has been the same as my approach to technology: to find a need and fill it. I benefited from the Boston community in practical, material ways, and I feel obligated to repay the community in practical, material ways. When we enter society at birth, we receive an inheritance from the people who lived before us. It is our responsibility to augment that inheritance for those who succeed us. I feel that all of us owe the world more than we received when we were born.

Recently I had the honor of being awarded the Medal of Liberty. The award, which was given during ceremonies marking the relighting of the Statue of Liberty, celebrated twelve Americans who had been born abroad but who had made their mark in America. Apart from myself, the group included Elie Wiesel, a survivor of the Holocaust; the architect, I. M. Pei; Dr. Albert Sabin, the inventor of the oral polio vaccine; and Irving Berlin, the composer. It is a mark of the generosity of the American spirit that the nation would choose to honor the contributions of its newest rather than its oldest citizens. While American society is by no means perfect, in its opportunities it is almost unique on this planet, and thus the key element in my accomplishments, and also, I believe, something to be cherished.

For many people, their schooling or their work stands in contrast to their outside lives—a price you pay in order to get to do the things you really want to do. I do not recognize that distinction. My education, my research at the Harvard Computation Laboratory, and my career, starting and building Wang Laboratories, have all been enormous fun. My days are spent doing the things I really want to do. The satisfaction of turning an idea into something real never diminishes, and the great gift of change is that it continually replenishes the stock of new ideas that might be brought to life. The thrill of this challenge more than compensates for the setbacks that are the price of learning and growth.

There are still many lessons to be learned.

Eugene Linden began his writing career as an investigative reporter in Vietnam in 1971. Since then, he has written on a wide range of subjects for a variety of publications. His other books are:

Apes, Men and Language
The Alms Race: The Impact of American Voluntary Aid Abroad
Affluence and Discontent: The Anatomy of Consumer Society
The Education of Koko (coauthored with Penny Patterson)
Silent Partners: The Legacy of the Ape Language Experiments

Index